T0267237

Favorite Flies for

COLORADO

50 ESSENTIAL PATTERNS FROM LOCAL EXPERTS

PAT DORSEY

STACKPOLE
BOOKS

Guilford, Connecticut
Blue Ridge Summit, Pennsylvania

STACKPOLE BOOKS

An imprint of Globe Pequot, the trade division of
The Rowman & Littlefield Publishing Group, Inc.
4501 Forbes Blvd., Ste. 200
Lanham, MD 20706
www.rowman.com

Distributed by NATIONAL BOOK NETWORK

Fly photographs by Brent Taylor
Photographs by the author unless noted

British Library Cataloguing in Publication Information available

Library of Congress Cataloging-in-Publication Data available

ISBN 978-0-8117-7032-3 (hardcover)
ISBN 978-0-8117-7033-0 (electronic)

♾™ The paper used in this publication meets the minimum requirements
of American National Standard for Information Sciences—Permanence of
Paper for Printed Library Materials, ANSI/NISO Z39.48-1992.

To Dad: Thanks for teaching me how to fly fish.
I am forever grateful that you gave me the gift of the outdoors
and taught me so many valuable lessons in Trout Country.
Without your guidance, none of this would be possible.
Not a day goes by that I don't think about you and the
adventures we shared. I love you dad; rest in peace!

CONTENTS

ACKNOWLEDGMENTS

As the title of this book implies, *Favorite Flies for Colorado: 50 Essential Patterns from Local Experts* is a group effort that shares decades of knowledge from some of the best fly tiers and anglers in the United States. It has been a distinct pleasure to work with some of the top industry professionals amassing this amazing collection of flies. I am confident that these proven patterns, recipes, and tying tips, as well as the tactics and techniques to fish them, will be appreciated by all.

Brent Taylor, thank you for your amazing fly photography. Your stunning images at the beginning of each chapter are the backbone of this book, allowing fly tiers of all abilities to re-create these beautiful flies. I'm happy that we could intertwine your passion for photography (profession) and fly tying into this joint venture.

I want to express my deepest gratitude to Jay Nichols for his support over the years. Thanks for all your hard work organizing, editing, and having the vision to produce this book. I greatly appreciate all your photo coaching and other tips along the way. I would also like to thank Judith Schnell and the team of professionals at Stackpole Books for their efforts.

Forrest Dorsey, thank you for submitting some of your beautiful pictures for this project. Your images are a nice addition to these pages; thanks for sharing your expertise behind the lens. I really appreciate all your other streamside efforts: help with head shots, fly photos, and your assistance carrying camera gear in the field to capture these images.

Landon Mayer, thanks for your continued support, supplemental images, and great content. I really appreciate your willingness to help out with this project.

A special thank-you to Brent Bauer and Russell Miller from Umpqua Feather Merchants for their assistance behind the scenes. You were always there to help dig up some history, cross-reference tying recipes, and provide contact information for many of these tiers. Your hard work and attention to detail are greatly appreciated.

Finally, none of this would be possible without the support of my wife, Kim. She has been by my side through thick and thin and is always there to encourage me. I appreciate your patience and understanding throughout this project.

INTRODUCTION

I tied my first fly with my uncle Jim Cantrall when I was 10 years old. Under his guidance, he taught me how to tie a Gray Hackle Yellow, which was a Dorsey family favorite back in the mid-1970s. After I got proficient at tying a Gray Hackle Yellow, we moved on to other patterns, including a Swayback Ant, Renegade, Orange Asher, and Brown Hackle Peacock. These were all proven favorites that my uncle, grandfather, and dad used on their excursions to the Eagle, Arkansas, South Platte, Roaring Fork, Blue, Gunnison, Taylor, and East Rivers. They were also effective on the Black Lakes, two stillwater impoundments on the top of Vail Pass, which my father, Jim Dorsey, and I frequented on a regular basis.

After several tying sessions in my uncle's basement, my father helped me purchase a Thompson Model A Vise, scissors, whip finisher, thread, wire, hooks, and myriad materials so I could begin experimenting on my own. My neighbor Brian Phillips was kind enough to lend me his copy of Jack Dennis's *Western Fly Tying Manual* (Volume 1), which helped me take my fly-tying abilities to the next level.

From the beginning I knew there was something special about the craft. Tying, designing, and collecting flies quickly became a passion that has lasted a lifetime. It didn't take me long to figure out that fooling a trout on a fly that I tied or designed was one of the most rewarding parts of fly fishing. With that being said, many fly fishers never tie their own flies (and that's okay), but they share a similar sense of accomplishment and satisfaction by choosing the appropriate fly during the height of a hatch or breaking the code when nothing else is working by thinking outside the box. All of these experiences are extremely rewarding—whether you tie your own or purchase your flies, you can never have too many! I've never met an auto mechanic with too many tools—and I have never come across an angler with too many flies. It's simply impossible!

Growing up in Colorado gave me the opportunity to mix and mingle with some of the best fly tiers and anglers in the country. I routinely hung out at Anglers All Ltd. and learned so many tricks of the trade from Bill Shappel, Terry and Lori Nicholson, Bob Kanaar, Doug Eccher, Nick Arndt, and Dick Mill. They were always willing to help out and share their time-tested patterns, techniques, and advice to help me improve my game.

Many of the country's top-producing fly patterns were designed by consummate anglers to fool selective trout on the state's world-class tailwaters, especially the Frying Pan and South Platte Rivers. Patterns like the South Platte Brassie, RS 2, WD-40, Buckskin, Miracle Nymph, Poor Witch, Disco Midge, Muskrat Nymph, Black Beauty, and Biot Midge were designed to fool selective trout on Colorado's renowned tailwaters. Their reputation and effectiveness for fooling finicky, hard-fished trout spread all over the country, where other tailwater junkies reaped the benefits of these patterns on their home waters.

It didn't stop there, as a new wave of talented tiers surfaced in the 1980s when Umpqua Feather Merchants started their royalty tier program. Anglers throughout the country could be part of this legacy by purchasing flies that were designed by some of the top industry professionals, many from Colorado, like John Betts, A. K. Best, Shane Stalcup, and Roy Palm, to name only a few. Today a number of fly manufacturers (like Umpqua Feather Merchants, Solitude Fly Company, Montana Fly Company, Orvis, and Fulling Mill) have a strong representation from Colorado, where these companies re-create flies to the tiers' exact specifications, distributing them nationwide. The book you are holding in your hands features many of these talented tiers, but due to space restraints, I could not feature all the gifted fly designers in Colorado.

With all the modern-day advancements, designing flies is more than using natural furs and feathers—innovation is spurred by the use of a wide array of synthetic materials into a fly tier's design. John Betts was on

Favorite Flies for Colorado: 50 Essential Patterns from Local Experts showcases everything from proven producers that have withstood the test of time to new, cutting-edge patterns like Landon Mayer's Mini Leech. Mayer's Mini Leech, like so many of the other flies featured in these pages, is available to consumers at specialty fly shops.

the leading edge of using synthetic materials that started in the early 1970s. He'll always be remembered as "Mr. Synthetic," as he was instrumental in using such products as Z-Lon, Zing Wing, Betts's Tailing Fibers, sparkle organza, Tyvek, Furry Foam, and many more in the design of his flies.

Creativity is now unleashed through experimentation and watching the way synthetic materials behave in the water, designing flies that breathe life, sink faster, float better, remain durable, and, most of all, consistently fool selective fish under a wide range of conditions. Charlie Craven's innovation is a great example. "While I have always loved natural materials, I find myself using more and more synthetics these days. Their consistency, availability, and durability make them an easy choice when you are trying to produce several of the same pattern. It surprises me how often I develop a new pattern then realize upon its completion that it is entirely synthetic except for a hackle feather or some deer hair."

While I personally tie the bulk of my own flies, I purchase a few from time to time, and have collected plenty of flies over the years from well-known fly tiers. I have two dozen RS 2s tied by Rim Chung and a couple dozen Breadcrust tied by Ed Rolka that I'll treasure for a lifetime. I also have several dozen of my uncle Jim's flies stashed away that have a tremendous amount of sentimental value. I continue to collect flies from influential fly designers that I've had the opportunity to work with over the years.

From a fly tier's perspective, it's fun to reminisce and look at some of my uncle's or grandfather's flies and look at the advancements that have been made in hooks, thread, wire, and so many other materials, especially the quality of hackle. The progression of the hackle industry in the past 30 years has simply been mindboggling. One of the biggest eye-opening experiences for me as a professional tier was taking a tour through Whiting Farms in Delta, Colorado. Dr. Tom Whiting personally took a group of select industry professionals on a private tour of his hackle operation. It was one of the most amazing experiences of my life. We got to watch chicks hatch, then we went through his facility and looked at thousands of birds. We had the opportunity to take a sneak peek at the drying room and how hackle is graded, packaged, and distributed worldwide. Dr. Whiting touches every bird personally from start to finish, which is pretty amazing to me.

Dr. Whiting was kind enough to share this historical information. "Modern dry-fly hackle occupies a unique position in the pantheon of tying materials—for it is both man-made and natural at the same time. Roosters grow the feathers, naturally, but only because man selectively bred them to do so, provided them the necessary environment, and then devised ways to process these natural feathers. These creations of man—the hackle rooster and the dry fly—allow the connection of many elements: man, bird, fish, and water. This is what fly fishing is fundamentally about—being in intimate connection with our natural world. The breeding and production of these very specialized lines of roosters has been an endeavor over the last 100 years by a host of individuals. The early pioneers are, most notably, Harry Darbee and his successor, Andy Miner Jr. Then the next generation of individuals who materially expanded and improved the lines in the 1960s, '70s, and '80s—to name only a few: Hoffman, Metz, and Hebert, who brought 'genetic hackle' to new levels of quality and availability. When I stumbled onto and into the 'hackle endeavor,' I discovered a truly interesting challenge that suited my nature and search for a long-term breeding project. My principle goals are to continuously improve

Fly tiers worldwide reap the benefits of Dr. Tom Whiting's genetic hackle lines. Over the past three decades, Whiting Farms has taken the hackle industry to the next level. Feathers are longer and thinner than anyone could have ever imagined. CURTIS FRY

the lines and be a responsible steward of them so they may continue in their noble partnership with fishing and be passed on for further development for generations to come."

Favorite Flies for Colorado: 50 Essential Patterns from Local Experts is a nice assortment of "oldies but goodies," historical patterns, proven favorites, and new cutting-edge, trending flies driven by modern innovation. Several old standbys, like the Woolly Bugger, Hare's Ear, Pheasant Tail, Royal Wulff, Humpy, Elk Hair Caddis, Irresistible, Comparadun (Sparkle Dun), Royal Coachman, Adams, Rio Grande King, Coachman Trude, Renegade, Gray Hackle Yellow, Brown Hackle Peacock, Orange Asher, Griffith's Gnat, San Juan Worm, Glo-Bug, Prince Nymph, Halfback Nymph, Twenty Incher, Miracle Nymph, Disco Midge, Muskrat Nymph, Biot Midge, and so on, are not included in these pages, but that doesn't mean they are not among the greatest trout flies of all time. Nothing could be further from the truth—in fact, all of the previously mentioned flies should be carried in everyone's fly box, as they play a vital role in fooling selective trout and matching the hatch throughout the state of Colorado.

My intent for *Favorite Flies for Colorado: 50 Essential Patterns from Local Experts* was to produce a compelling book that showcases the wealth of knowledge and talent in Colorado. In a few cases I've included patterns by anglers that reside in other locations, but they grew up in Colorado or visit the Centennial State on a regular basis. The project began by reaching out to several tiers in Colorado and asking them to submit one or two of their favorite flies, which creates a unique project with a flavor of its own.

The word "favorite" is subjective and can be interpreted in a number of ways, by both the tier and the reader. Some tiers imply their favorite pattern was the fly they caught their first fish on, while others say it was a fly that their father or grandfather used, or an artificial imposter they designed out of a necessity to fill a niche or match the hatch. One of my favorite flies is the Renegade, a dry fly that my father and I fished in the Gunnison Valley when I was growing up. Every time I see a Renegade or tie one, it reignites those childhood memories. The possibilities are endless—that's what makes this book project different, fun, and a breath of fresh air.

What I am trying to avoid is rehashing old information and patterns that have been written about over and over again in other books and publications for decades. Once again, with limited space, I can only feature a certain number of patterns from any one individual. Master fly tiers like John Barr, Charlie Craven, Rick Takahashi, Greg Garcia, Landon Mayer, Juan Ramirez, Richard Pilatzke, and so many

more could easily fill these pages with their time-tested patterns.

The good news is each one of the previously mentioned tiers is part of this project, along with so many other talented individuals, including Steve Henderson, Matt Miles, Forrest Dorsey, Jim Cannon, Rim Chung, A. K. Best, Shane Stalcup, Dick Shinton, Mike Kruise, Phil Iwane, Ben Furimsky, Greg Blessing, Son Tao, Joe Shafer, Ed Rolka, Don Puterbaugh, Jack Dennis, Matt Bennett, Chris Johnson, Herman deGala, Matt McCannel, Chris Krueger, Steve Maldonado, Eric Pettine, Tim Heng, Michael Gula, Al Ritt, Aaron Carithers, Mark Engler, Carl Pennington, John Betts, Jim Poor, Rick Yancik, Brian Kelso, Steve Thomas, Gene Lynch, Ken Chandler, Tug Davenport, and Ed Marsh.

Narrowing down the list to fifty flies was no easy task—in fact it was extremely difficult! I feel it's important to have a nice representation of midges, mayflies, caddisflies, and stoneflies, as well as other important food organisms, including forage items, terrestrials, scuds, and mysis shrimp. *Favorite Flies for Colorado: 50 Essential Patterns from Local Experts* caters to a wide audience, from stillwater enthusiasts to anglers that prefer to fish rivers and streams. Furthermore, I've included patterns that work well for a variety of gamefish including trout, bass, carp, muskie, bluegills, crappie, and pike. As an added bonus, many patterns have crossover applications. For instance, John Barr's Meat Whistle consistently fools trout, bass, carp, and pike. Matt Bennett's Lunch Money is also a versatile pattern with the same goals in mind that every angler should carry in a wide range of sizes and colors.

Each chapter includes a photograph of the featured fly, including the tying recipe and the history of each pattern. I feel it's important to discuss pattern variations, which helps cross-pollinate so many wonderful patterns, and

Jim Cannon's contribution to the fly-fishing world for the past 35 years has been impressive to say the least. As a fly shop owner, guide, and instructor, he's educated the masses on tying flies to fool selective trout. Cannon is known for his Snowshoe Dun series, which is all-inclusive of blue-winged olives, pale morning duns, and Tricos (pictured from left to right). This group of mayflies is referred to as the "Big Three" by spring creek and tailwater enthusiasts. BRENT TAYLOR

give credit where credit is due. For instance, the RS 2 and its numerous variations are all important. Rim Chung invented the pattern in the 1970s, but innovative tiers improved the original pattern in so many ways. Each variation has a time and place and should be part of everyone's arsenal of flies. I've included a full chapter devoted to the RS 2 and its variations.

In most cases the pictured fly is tied by the original designer, which lends so much credibility to the project. Each tier unveils what spurred their innovation, what tying materials they use and why, tying tips, and, most of all, how they recommend fishing their patterns. Having the appropriate fly is only part of the equation for success—knowing how to fish it is equally important. Each tier has been willing to give back and share so much

information that benefits us all. I've taken the liberty to tie some of the historical patterns and flies from those amazing anglers and fly tiers that have passed away or I have lost contact with over the years. In a few instances, I've relied on fly manufacturers to assist me in filling in a few of the holes so that every fly is represented correctly.

My goals and objectives for *Favorite Flies for Colorado: 50 Patterns from Local Experts* will have been met if you somehow benefit from the words, pictures, and tying recipes on these pages. I am hopeful that you will enjoy the delightful blend of history, tying tips, modern-day innovation, and some solid fishing advice from some of the best anglers in the state of Colorado. Hopefully many of these patterns end up in your fly boxes and prove to be some of your favorite flies for Colorado.

AC's Ant

(Tied by Aaron Carithers)

- **Hook:** #16–#20 Tiemco 100
- **Thread:** Black 8/0
- **Body:** Black 2 mm craft foam
- **Underbody:** Peacock herl and grizzly hackle
- **Wing:** Tan EP fibers
- **Legs:** Black Hareline Midge Tubing, knotted to create joints

Aaron Carithers is one of the fishiest guys I know. Born in Wheat Ridge, Colorado, and raised in the nearby community of Arvada, his family goes back five generations in the Front Range. Carithers's grandfather introduced him to fly fishing when he was 7 years old, fishing the Little Michigan in North Park and moving on to the Big Thompson, Cache la Poudre, and St. Vrain as he got older. After he got his driver's license, he began exploring Bear Creek and the South Platte River on his own. It wasn't long after that he was driving across the western United States in search of places to fish.

"After graduating from Arvada West High School in 1987, I spent a brief time learning to row whitewater boats on the North Platte near the Colorado-Wyoming border and on to the Salmon River in Idaho, training with Jim Temple and the guides of Ways West Adventures. Unfortunately, the season was an extreme low-water year and nearly all of the trips were canceled, cutting my whitewater career short. I decided I had better go to college; my criteria included close year-round fly fishing and a rugby team. Fort Lewis College in Durango, Colorado, seemed to be the best fit."

AC's Ant is a versatile terrestrial pattern that works well for imitating small black-bodied ants as well as larger varieties like the carpenter ant. Aaron Carithers also likes to think outside the box from time to time and use his ant pattern to unmatch the hatch during the height of a midge emergence.

After fishing several days a week on the Animas, San Juan, Dolores, and the numerous mountain creeks, Carithers decided to accept a guide position with Jerry Freeman, owner of Anasazi Angler Guide Service. "I worked for Jerry Freeman for five seasons, guiding mostly on the San Juan River. In need of a little variety, I went to work for Duranglers, guiding the San Juan as well as the Piedra, Animas, Rio Grande, Dolores, Lime, and Cascade creeks. After working six seasons for Duranglers, I wanted to expand my profession and control my own destiny. In 1998 I purchased Anasazi Angler and have owned it ever since."

I've had the opportunity to fish with Carithers on numerous occasions. It didn't take me long to figure out that he is a passionate dry-fly angler. "I moved from the Front Range to Durango, not only to attend Fort Lewis College but to dry-fly fish in the hundreds of miles of creek water flowing from the San Juan Mountains. AC's Ant has been one of my go-to patterns for the area's creeks, freestones, and tailwaters. It works well for imitating

Durango-based fishing guide Aaron Carithers is always looking for rising fish. Whether he is working on one of his local streams or fishing the nearby San Juan River in northern New Mexico, AC's Ant is one of his go-to dry flies.

small black ants, but where it really shines is in unmatching the hatch."

The San Juan River provides anglers with some of the best dry-fly fishing in the West. "Midges are the primary food source for the San Juan River's rainbows and browns, but the dry-fly fishing with a single adult can be very frustrating. The midge feeders often eat a size 24 or 26 Parachute Adams, but it can be difficult to see, especially in harsh glare or foam lines. Over the years I have found that a small black-bodied dry fly such as the Peacock Caddis fools most selective adult midge eaters, but after one 'eat' the fly usually loses its buoyancy and sinks. This makes it hard to distinguish it from other debris in a foam line. That is the main reason I developed AC's Ant, to solve this problem. My goals and objectives were simple: I wanted to create a pattern that would consistently fool midge feeders, be easy to see, and be extremely durable."

AC's Ant is also effective fished out of a drift boat on the upper Rio Grande. "As the float season progresses and the larger stoneflies become less frequent, the Rio Grande browns and rainbows key in on small black-bodied caddis. AC's Ant fished alone is a great boat fly. It floats well and is also deadly for black caddis."

Carithers has enjoyed a lot of success with AC's Ant on the Dolores River as well. "During a PMD hatch, I like to use a stealthy approach and rig an AC's Ant trailed by a size 18 Floating PMD Nymph because the small foam ant pattern makes a great indicator. Dry and dropper rigs are always a great alternative after the fish have been pounded all summer. I was really surprised to find out that the picky trout on the Dolores frequently prefer the small terrestrial pattern over the trailing floating nymph."

AC's Ant also works well for imitating carpenter ants. Carithers recommends tying AC's Ant in a size 16 to imitate carpenter ants.

- **Hook:** #4–#8 Tiemco 5263
- **Thread:** Brown 6/0 Uni-Thread
- **Abdomen:** Olive Krystal Chenille
- **Hackle:** Brown rooster
- **Underbody:** Tan 2 mm craft foam
- **Overbody:** Brown 2 mm craft foam
- **Legs:** Brown rubber legs (medium)
- **Underwing:** Rainbow Krystal Flash
- **Wing:** Light elk hair
- **Thorax:** Arizona Peacock Dubbing
- **Wing case:** Overbody foam pulled back and tied down
- **Indicator:** Orange 2 mm craft foam

Amy's Ant

(Tied by Jack Dennis)

Master angler and fly tier Jack Dennis developed Amy's Ant in the mid-1990s. Although Dennis spent a large part of his professional career in Jackson, Wyoming, he is no stranger to Colorado. As a young man, he attended sixth grade through his junior year in high school in Colorado, where he frequented many of Colorado's renowned fisheries. He spent his summers with his grandfather in Jackson, where he eventually opened his fly shop, Jack Dennis Outdoor Shop. Dennis cultivated strong relationships with outdoor legends like Hank Roberts, Jim Poor, and Chuck

Fothergill because he spent a lot of his spare time fishing in Colorado.

Amy's Ant is a Colorado favorite for imitating adult golden stoneflies because it fools hard-fished trout under a wide range of conditions. While the name "Amy's Ant" might sound misleading for an adult stonefly imitation, trust me—this pattern is essential in stonefly-ridden waters.

According to Dennis, his wife and former vice president Dick Cheney inspired him to tie this fly for the famous Jackson Hole One Fly competition. Prior to designing the fly, Dennis

Jack Dennis's Amy's Ant imitates a variety of food organisms, but it works best as a golden stonefly adult during the summer months. Whether you're trying to match the hatch or looking to fool an opportunistic feeder, Amy's Ant does it all. Amy's Ant is easy to see, floats high on riffled currents, and fools trout that are feeding both selectively and opportunistically.

asked several guides in the Jackson area for their input on how they would improve the famed Chernobyl Ant. James Osborne, head guide of Heise Outfitters, among several other colleagues, offered their input. Per Dennis, "It was really everybody's fly, as I borrowed a suggestion or two from a multitude of friends to craft the final product."

After a group consensus, one of the biggest problems with the Chernobyl Ant was that it lacked a wing to imitate the natural movement of an adult stonefly. Taking suggestions from veteran guides, Dennis decided to design an underwing made from rainbow Krystal Flash, which would glow from the light through the water to imitate the fluttering effect of a stonefly's wings. Dennis later added a tan elk hair wing on the top of the Krystal Flash to add buoyancy, coupled with pulling the frontal foam back into the thorax area to form a wing case. This produced a durable fly that would float like a cork and ride high on fast, oxygenated currents.

Dennis says, "The best judge was the fish. We caught an amazing number of fish the first time we started fishing the fly. It won the One Fly competition in 1999 and quickly became Vice President Cheney's favorite fly." Dennis later named it Amy's Ant, after his daughter.

Monroe Coleman, a veteran guide of 25-plus years for the Blue Quill Angler in Evergreen, Colorado, popularized Amy's Ant in Colorado, specifically in Cheesman Canyon, where there is a dense population of golden stoneflies. Word spread quickly, and Amy's Ant has become a favorite dry fly on the Blue, Colorado, Eagle, Roaring Fork, Gunnison, and many other Colorado rivers.

I recommend concentrating your efforts around darker areas in the substrate, and focus hard on shallow riffles on the stream bank. Especially target sections close to logs, cliff faces, and partially submerged structures,

where stoneflies routinely fall into the water. Fishing water that is 2 to 4 feet deep will produce the best results. Both dead-drifted and skated presentations fool trout, but I typically dead-drift Amy's Ant most of the time.

One of the most challenging aspects of fishing large dry flies is setting the hook prematurely. Allow the trout to come up, eat your fly, and dip its head below the surface before you gently lift the rod tip to set the hook. If you react too early, you may come away empty-handed. If you miss your target, the chances are pretty good you spoiled your opportunity. However, I have observed cases where I have switched to a red Amy's Ant and enticed the trout to eat again.

Dry and droppers are another effective method of fishing Amy's Ant. One of my favorite rigs is fishing Amy's Ant with a #18-to-#20 Mercer's Micro Mayfly or Mitchell's Split Case BWO. I typically drop 18 to 24 inches of tippet material off the bend of the hook and attach my dropper fly. This allows anglers to fish a wide assortment of water, including shallow bank water, transitional zones that funnel into deep pools, riffles, runs, and pocket water.

This Cheesman Canyon rainbow wasted no time eating an Amy's Ant during a golden stonefly emergence. Amy's Ant is also a great choice if you opt to fish with a dry-and-dropper rig, as it supports a variety of small bead heads without any compromise.

ARF Humpulator

(Tied by Al Ritt)

■ **Hook:** #6–#10 Partridge CS 42 Bomber
■ **Tail:** Tan calf tail
■ **Underbody:** Tan closed-cell foam (leave tag end extending past the rear of the hook)
■ **Abdomen:** Yellow polypropylene yarn
■ **Rear hackle:** Brown Whiting Farms rooster
■ **Shell back:** Tag end of the tan foam underbody
■ **Underwing:** Opal Mirage flash
■ **Wing:** Tan MFC Widows Web
■ **Indicator:** Fluorescent orange Para-Post yarn
■ **Head:** Peacock Ice Dub
■ **Front hackle:** Grizzly dyed brown Whiting Farms rooster

If you enjoy floating one of Colorado's mighty freestones during the summer months, you know the importance of carrying a thorough selection of large attractor dry flies. One thing is for certain though—all dry flies are not created equal! Some patterns float exceptionally well and can withstand the punishment of bouncing off rocks, hanging up in overhanging brush and trees, and, most important, the abuse dished out by the trout's teeth. In contrast, many flies get waterlogged quickly and sink, which is a huge problem when you're float fishing.

Anglers that fish out of drift boats and inflatable rafts must rely upon maintenance-free patterns to maximize their fishing time. Al Ritt

Al Ritt's ARF Humpulator is the perfect candidate for float anglers who enjoy pounding the stream banks with large dry flies. There is nothing more frustrating than a fly that sinks. Ritt's concoction was designed to float on the choppiest of western waterways to eliminate this problem. By changing the color scheme, the ARF Humpulator can be hatch-specific (e.g., orange for salmon flies, yellow for golden stones, and so on), or the ARF Humpulator can be fished as an attractor.

sums it up well: "I remember my first float trip vividly—much anticipation preceded it. I had floated smaller and lower-gradient streams, for coldwater, warmwater, and anadromous species, but this was my first trip down a 'classic' western river that required a legitimate drift boat with someone on the oars the entire trip. We met our guide in Basalt, a small town in Colorado where the Frying Pan River merges with the Roaring Fork River. Before launching, our guide spent a few minutes briefing us on what the day would look like. We chatted about the bugs we might encounter, rigging, and where the fish were likely to be. Next we discussed something I had not considered. Float trips like we were about to partake in require a guide's undivided attention to line the boat up for good drifts and to be safe at all times. In Colorado if you are floating through private property, you are not allowed to anchor or touch the stream bottom. So we learned quickly, the more we could do ourselves, and the faster we could do it, the more fishing we would enjoy."

Every day on the water is a learning experience, and this day was no different. This outing is what led Ritt to come up with a fly he calls the ARF Humpulator. "On my inaugural float trip we fished large foam grasshopper patterns with deer-hair wings. They were slathered in floatant and dipped in dry-fly crystals. They looked like giant dandelion seeds and they floated beautifully . . . for a while. But eventually they got waterlogged, no matter how much desiccate we used," he said.

Upon returning home, Ritt began working on a pattern that would perform better. "I like the versatility of patterns like a Stimulator that can be used to mimic several different insects or function as an attractor. A Stimulator has the reputation for floating well but not as well as I wanted." Ritt began working on a pattern similar to a Stimulator but added a foam strip over the back of the abdomen to increase floatation. The next area of concern was the wing. "Deer hair floats well initially, but in time water penetrates it, replacing the air in the interior cells and causing the fly to sink."

Ritt's next batch of flies used calf tail (instead of deer hair), but he faced similar challenges. Ritt decided to use Montana Fly Company's Widow's Web for the wing because it does not absorb water. "The final detail was a material I feel is underutilized today—polypropylene yarn. I substituted the yarn for the dubbed body because it is actually lighter than water. Besides adding floatation, this reduced my tying time. Last came some aesthetic components: an Opal Mirage underwing to imitate a fluttering effect, and an indicator to help locate the fly in choppy water or harsh glare."

The most effective method to fish an ARF Humpulator is with a 9-foot leader terminating in 3X or 4X tippet. The best rule of thumb is to fish with the largest tippet you can and still get strikes. When you are using large, beefy dry flies, the trout are rarely leader-shy. Ritt recommends changing up the colors and sizes to imitate hoppers, golden stoneflies, salmon flies, yellow sallies, and larger varieties of caddisflies.

Al Ritt's ARF Humpulator was designed with a float fisherman in mind. Ritt's design is brilliant because the ARF Humpulator is extremely durable and easy to see, floats high on the choppiest of currents, and supports dropper flies if you opt to use one.

Autumn Splendor

(Tied by Tim Heng)

- **Hook:** #6–#10 Tiemco 5263
- **Weight:** .20 lead wire
- **Thread:** Brown 6/0 Uni-Thread
- **Tail:** Brown marabou with copper Krystal Flash
- **Abdomen:** Brown chenille (medium)
- **Legs:** Yellow round rubber legs
- **Rib:** Copper Ultra Wire (small)
- **Hackle:** Orange and yellow dyed grizzly

Tim Heng has been a fixture in the Roaring Fork Valley for the past 40 years. Heng moved from Denver to Glenwood Springs in January of 1978 and began tying flies commercially for a small fly shop called the Ginger Quill that was located at the Ranch of the Roaring Fork. He tied for them for a year or so before they went out of business. That was Heng's first venture in commercial tying, and it ultimately led him into a successful career in the fly-fishing industry.

In the fall of 1981, Heng and his good friend Lars Anderberg opened Roaring Fork Anglers, Glenwood Springs' first specialty fly shop. "We went into the business more with our heart and love of fly fishing than with good business sense and, more important, capital. I was tying a majority of the flies that we were selling during those times. At that time we were one of only a small handful of people who were floating the area waters commercially with drift boats. In those days the water quality of the Roaring Fork was not near what it is today, and because of that it didn't have near the fish population we currently enjoy. It was not until the 1983 season, when what was then the Colorado Division of Wildlife labeled the Roaring Fork a Gold Medal fishery from

Heng's original Autumn Splendor has been one of Colorado's favorite streamers for the past three decades. In recent years cone-head, bead-head, and dumbbell-eye variations have become popular too.

the Crystal River downstream to the confluence of the Colorado River, that the fishery started to improve."

In 1985 Heng and Anderberg sold Roaring Fork Anglers to Carl Maulbautch. "Carl asked me to stay on and manage Roaring Fork Anglers, so I did for the next 5 years. I also started guiding a lot more during that time." Heng quickly earned the reputation of being one of valley's premier float guides on the Roaring Fork and Colorado Rivers.

In 1988 Heng developed the Autumn Splendor. He was guiding a client on the Roaring Fork River on a particularly slow early fall day. "We had tried several different nymphs, dries, and streamers with very limited success when my client asked if he could try one of his flies that he used in Texas for largemouth bass. When he first showed it to me, I thought there is no way this fly will work. It was tied on a 2/0 hook, had doll eyes the size of my thumbnail, and had a brown, yellow, and orange body with white rubber legs. Surely no self-respecting trout on the Roaring Fork River would have any interest in it. But because it was so slow, I thought let's give it a

Tim Heng's Autumn Splendor has long been one of Colorado's top-producing streamers. This is a variation of the original pattern that incorporates dumbbell eyes into the design to help it sink quickly.

try for a short period of time. Well, as you can probably imagine, we started seeing fish move on it. I don't think we ever actually hooked a fish on the fly, but for the next hour or so, we saw fish chase it, turn on it, maybe run from it, but it definitely garnered their attention."

There was something magical about the fly, so Heng decided he would scale it back in size and add a few more "trout features" to it. "First I tied it on a #4 streamer hook and put a brown marabou tail with copper-colored crystal flash. Then I put lead wire on it and tied three yellow rubber legs sticking out girdle-bug style. I covered the body with brown chenille, and for hackle I used one yellow dyed grizzly saddle and one orange dyed grizzly saddle and palmered them down the body. I then counter-wrapped the hackle with fine copper wire to give it strength. A couple of days later, I was back on the water with a different client and we gave the new fly a try. This time instead of just looking at the fly, they ate it, and ate it, and ate it! It truly amazed me how well it worked. So I said to my client, 'what do you think I should call it?' and he came up with the name Autumn Splendor."

Heng has since caught largemouth and smallmouth bass, crappie, bluegills, and carp on the Autumn Splendor. Heng originally tied the Autumn Splendor without a cone, but the copper cone-head version is most popular today. "I generally fish it with short strips, but it can also be effective with a dead drift or crawled slowly along the bottom for bass and carp."

In 1990 Heng was offered the manager's job at Taylor Creek in Basalt by Bill Fitzsimmons and continued to work there for the next 27 years.

Heng has retired from his shop duties but still does the occasional guide trip for Taylor Creek Fly Shop. He spends his summers in the Roaring Fork Valley and winters in Mexico.

- **Hook:** #10–#14 MFC 7073 3XL Bent Shank
- **Bead:** MFC Coffee lucent tungsten
- **Thread:** 6/0 yellow Uni-Thread
- **Underbody:** Flat lead tape
- **Tail:** Goldstone goose biots
- **Abdomen:** Light-golden stone Hareline D-Rib (medium) wrapped over yellow thread
- **Markers:** Desert-tan Chartpak and Sharpie brown. Top side of abdomen colored on thread before D-Rib is wrapped.
- **Legs:** Hungarian partridge
- **Wing case:** Golden stone Rainey's Stretch Flex (⅛")
- **Thorax:** Tannish yellow Rene Harrop's dubbing mixed with light-yellow UV Ice Dub Mix 70% tannish yellow, 30% light-yellow UV Ice Dub

Bead Head D-Rib Golden Stonefly Nymph

(Tied by Carl Pennington)

A winter outing with Carl Pennington on the South Platte River near Deckers reminded me of the importance of golden stonefly nymphs as a year-round food source. It's easy to get trapped in an "out of sight, out of mind" mentality and overlook one of the most important food sources for trout simply based on not seeing anything hatching. On that winter day, I was trying to match the hatch with midge imitations while Pennington was thinking outside the box and catching a bunch of fish on his Bead Head D-Rib Golden Stonefly Nymph.

Savvy anglers know that golden stonefly imitations are productive year-round because of the nymph's multiyear life cycle. Golden stoneflies (*Calineuria pacifica*) live up to 3 years, so even after the adults have emerged for the season, several year classes remain plentiful in the stream's substrate. "I fish with my Bead Head D-Rib Golden Stonefly Nymph twelve months out of the year. I consistently

If you enjoy fishing with stoneflies, Carl Pennington's D-Rib Golden Stonefly Nymph is a pattern you'll want to include in your fly selection. I've witnessed the effectiveness of this pattern firsthand, both at Deckers and in Cheesman Canyon, and the results have been truly amazing.

fool trout with it, regardless of the conditions or the time of year," Pennington says.

Pennington's Bead Head D-Rib Golden Stonefly was designed for the South Platte River in Cheesman Canyon. "My goal was to create a golden stonefly nymph that could be tied in smaller sizes down to a 12 or 14. My seine samples showed there was a tremendous amount of immature stoneflies in that size range. I was also looking for a pattern that would have a definite color variation from top to bottom. Golden stoneflies range in color from golden brown to dark brown, with their underside being distinctly lighter than their topside."

Pennington's design is as realistic as they come. He begins with a forked tail made from goose biots, then uses flat lead tape to produce the abdomen. Pennington overlays the lead underbody with yellow thread, then uses a tan-and-brown marker to color the dorsal side of the abdomen with a nice mottled effect. Then he wraps D-Rib over the colored thread underbody to produce a beautiful segmented

This Cheesman Canyon rainbow ate one of Carl Pennington's Bead Head D-Rib Golden Stonefly Nymphs. Pennington was kind enough to give me a dozen of his Bead Head D-Rib Golden Stonefly Nymphs, so I put them to good use.

abdomen. Pennington recommends using a mixture of Rene Harrop's tannish-yellow dubbing combined with light-yellow UV Ice Dub for the thorax to simulate the gills. The legs are composed of Hungarian partridge, and the wing case is made from Rainey's Golden Stone Stretch Flex to match the coloration of the topside of the abdomen.

A great time to fish with a golden stonefly imitation is when the nymphs molt, passing through their final instar before reaching maturity. This typically occurs during the latter part of February into the first part of March. "If you can catch the golden stonefy nymphs while they are molting, it can be an epic day, one you won't forget about anytime soon." You'll know when the golden stoneflies are molting because you'll see a lot of golden stonefly exoskeletons drifting in the current; it's nearly impossible to miss.

Without a doubt, the best time of year to fish with golden stoneflies is the days leading up to the hatch, when the adults are migrating to the river's edge to emerge. Emergence occurs on land after the nymph crawls up on a rock, log, bridge abutment, tree trunk, or nearby structure to hatch into an adult. If you see several exoskeletons on the side of any of the previously mentioned areas, it's safe to assume the adults have hatched for the season.

"I typically fish the Bead Head D-Rib Golden Stonefly Nymph as the lead fly in a tandem three-fly nymph rig. I vary the size of the fly based on the time of year. In the wintertime I fish with a size 14, but during the spring, summer, and fall, I use size 10 or 12. I fish a rubber leg version when the water is off-colored and running high." Pennington's dropper flies are based on the current hatches at any given time. For instance, during the winter he'll trail midge imitations (larvae and pupae), during the shoulder seasons he uses *Baetis* nymphs (emergers), and so on.

Breadcrust

(Tied by Ed Rolka)

- **Hook:** #12–#18 Tiemco 5262
- **Thread:** Black 6/0 or 8/0 Uni-Thread
- **Underbody:** Brown yarn
- **Abdomen:** Red-phase ruffed grouse tail quill
- **Collar:** Grizzly hen

Rudy Sentiwany is credited with inventing the original Breadcrust in the Pocono Mountains (northeastern Pennsylvania) back in the early 1940s. Ed Rolka, a fellow Pennsylvanian, popularized the Breadcrust in Colorado. According to Rolka, "Not much history was available about the fly, but when I began fly fishing in 1950, the Breadcrust was the hot fly back East! Originally, the Breadcrust was called the Breadbasket because it had the reputation of quickly filling a basket (creel) with trout. When and why the name of the fly changed eludes me." My guess is that Rudy

Sentiwany was a grouse hunter, because the tail of the eastern red-phase ruffed grouse is used to tie the fly. I'm speculating that the fly's name changed from Breadbasket to Breadcrust because of its physical (crust-like) appearance.

Rolka tied the Breadcrust commercially and supplied fly shops and businesses all over the country, including the Orvis Company in Manchester, Vermont. In 1970 Rolka moved his family to Denver after he accepted a job with the Johns Manville Company. Upon his arrival he sent Bill Logan, outdoor editor at the *Rocky*

The famed Breadcrust was born in the Pocono Mountains in the early 1940s and later popularized by Ed Rolka in the Rockies in the 1970s. In Colorado the Breadcrust is one of the most popular cased caddis imitations because of its buggy appearance.

Mountain News, a few samples of the Breadcrust. Impressed with the fly, Logan wrote a story about the Breadcrust, focusing on two popular fishing destinations, the Roaring Fork and Frying Pan Rivers, which are known for their reliable caddis hatches.

"After the article came out in the Wednesday paper, I sold twenty dozen Breadcrust to Ken Walters down at The Flyfisher Ltd. in Cherry Creek. Walters had to reorder the next day because the Breadcrust were all gone," said Rolka. Word spread quickly, and soon fly shops all over the central Rocky Mountain region filled their fly bins with Breadcrust. Rolka continued to supply fly shops with Breadcrust for the next two decades.

In 1993 I sat next to Rolka at the annual West Denver Trout Unlimited Fly Tying Clinic. He mentioned he was ready to retire from fly tying and asked me if I was interested in tying the Breadcrust commercially and supplying fly shops in the Denver metro area. Well, that was a no-brainer, and it was my first huge break in the fly-fishing industry. I was honored to keep his tradition alive!

Mid-May is a great time to fish with a Bead Head Breadcrust on a freestone stream like the fabled Gunnison River. The Breadcrust and its variations can be dead-drifted underneath a strike indicator or swung in the current like a traditional wet fly.

Rolka was kind enough to unveil his trade secrets to tying a Breadcrust. Without a doubt, the preparation of the quill is the most difficult part to tying the fly. Rolka showed me how to trim the barbules, soak and split the grouse quill with a double-edge razor blade, and clean the pith from the center of the quill. Once the quill was prepared, tying the fly was easy. I quickly learned the importance of preparing a big batch of grouse tails ahead of time to speed up production. Within a month I began filling Breadcrust orders for twenty-plus fly shops throughout the Rockies.

Like other fly patterns, the Breadcrust evolved over time. There are several variations of the original pattern that I suggest you carry in your fly box. A bead-head version, both with tungsten and brass beads, is a nice alternative. The bead assists in a quick sink rate and also helps mimic the gas bubble effect during a caddisfly's emergence. Dying a red-phase ruffed grouse tail fan olive is another nice option, incorporating a matte-black tungsten bead with an olive grizzly hen collar.

I recommend fishing a Breadcrust with a standard two- or three-fly nymphing rig consisting of a 9-foot, 4X tapered leader trailing one or two flies to match any corresponding hatches. If you see midges buzzing around the stream, use a midge pupa; if you observe pale morning duns emerging, use a Barr Emerger (PMD); and so on. You may also opt to fish this pattern like a conventional, single wet fly, casting it down and across and allowing it to swing in the current. Another effective strategy is to fish a size 16-to-18 Bead Head Breadcrust under a buoyant dry fly such as a Puterbaugh Caddis, Elk-Hair Caddis, or Goddard Caddis. This strategy works well in slower pools when the trout are engaged and feeding heavily on caddis pupae. Observation is key—if you see several trout suspended and chasing pupae, I highly recommend this tactic.

Buckskin

(Tied by Pat Dorsey)

- **Hook:** #16–#20 Tiemco 100
- **Thread:** 8/0 black Uni-Thread
- **Tail:** Brown hen fibers
- **Body:** Chamois strip
- **Head:** Tying thread

Ed Marsh of Colorado Springs developed the Buckskin in 1972 to imitate the dense population of free-living caddis larvae that reside in the South Platte River. The original pattern was composed of a short brown hen hackle tail and a thin, tapered strip of tanned deer hide. Marsh wound the buckskin around the hook shank with the rough side out to create a segmented body. He used brown hen hackle near the head, tied in and swept back, to imitate the legs on the larva. The fly was finished off with a pronounced black thread head, a prominent feature of *Rhyacophila*.

Bob Saile, former outdoor editor for the *Denver Post*, showed me a different version in the early 1990s, a pattern he referred to as a Chamois Skin. It also had a brown hen hackle beard, similar to Marsh's design, but it did not have a tail. The biggest difference was the body was tied from a car chamois strip instead of tanned buckskin. The Chamois Skin was one of Saile's favorite patterns for the South Platte River near Deckers and Trumbull.

The version most anglers carry in their fly boxes today (pictured) is a combination of the two previously mentioned patterns. Tiers can

Don't let the simplicity of Ed Marsh's Buckskin fool you—it is one of the most dependable flies that you can use in Colorado. If your objective is to imitate a caddis larva on your favorite stream, it's hard to go wrong with a size-18 Buckskin.

choose whether or not they want to include a tail in their design. My guess is that the brown tail that was incorporated into Marsh's original design was to imitate the anal claws of a free-living caddis. The head is usually tied with black thread, but it's not uncommon to see dubbing or peacock herl used.

There are several other variations of the Buckskin that have surfaced over the years. Bill Grems, owner of Complete Anglers in Englewood, Colorado, came up with a bead-head version (tungsten and brass) that he tied on a Tiemco 2487 using tan 8/0 Uni-Thread. He wrapped the chamois strip around the curved hook shank (no tail), tied a small thread collar behind the bead, and called it good. In the mid-1990s I came up with the Mercury Buckskin, which is tied on a Tiemco 100 and has a brown tail like the original pattern, a strip of chamois for the body, peacock herl for the collar, and a silver-lined glass bead to imitate the highly reflective area of trapped gases in the thorax area prior to emergence.

Fellow industry professional Luke Bever came up with Bever's Better Buckskin in 2004. Bever uses a size 12-to-16 Tiemco 3761, 8/0 Black Uni-Thread, Ultrasuede for the abdomen, and the thorax is a mixture of peacock and black ostrich herl. He incorporates a backstrap of medium pearl Mylar tinsel and ribs the fly with small or Brassie-size UTC Ultra Wire, producing a super-realistic and durable caddis larva.

Charlie Craven featured Luke Bever's Better Buckskin in *Fly Fisherman* magazine. According to Craven, "Luke took this basic chassis and dressed it up a bit to make it match the real thing a bit 'better.' Starting with a strip of flashy pearl Mylar tinsel over the back of a twisted Ultrasuede body, he then created a more complicated yet lifelike head section that blends the fish-catching power and iridescence of peacock herl with the realism of

longer, flowing ostrich herl legs. Ribbed with copper wire for both durability and a bit of color, the end result is a pattern that is truly better than the original in every way. Luke fishes his pattern all year, and often fishes it along with an egg pattern during the winter and early spring. His subtle yet familiar caddis larva catches more than its share of fish that are shy of the more obvious egg."

I find a Buckskin works well dropped off an attractor like a San Juan Worm. I typically trail a Mercury Flashback Pheasant or Sparkle Wing RS 2 off the Buckskin. This rig has proven itself time and time again on the Williams Fork, Colorado, South Platte, Blue, Taylor, Gunnison, Eagle, Roaring Fork, and Yampa Rivers. Caddis larvae are an important year-round food source for trout, despite most anglers' "out of sight, out of mind" mentality. Don't get trapped into thinking caddis larvae are only effective during peak caddis emergence, as nothing could be further from the truth. Opportunistic trout are always aware of their presence and waste little time eating one if the opportunity presents itself.

A Buckskin is one of the most reliable producers along the South Platte corridor during the summer months. South Platte veterans like Brian Leen know how important it is to have an ample supply of Buckskins in sizes 16 to 20.

Bunny Sculpin

(Tied by Steve Henderson)

- **Hook:** #2–#4 Tiemco 9395
- **Thread:** Rusty-brown UTC 140-denier
- **Eyes:** Yellow and black lead eyes—size large on #4, extra large on #2
- **Belly:** Rust-brown Hareline bunny strip
- **Back:** Rust-brown Hareline bunny strip palmered at head
- **Lateral line:** Medium brown Krystal Flash
- **Pectoral fins:** Yellow Hareline bunny strip

I met Steve Henderson 25 years ago at a Trout Unlimited Meeting in Steamboat Springs. The following day he took me out fishing on the Yampa River, and we've been friends ever since. It didn't take me long to figure out that Steve Henderson had an uncanny ability to fool fish with streamers.

A day on the Yampa River with Henderson never disappoints—it's always jam-packed with many valuable lessons and plenty of opportunities to catch some beautiful fish. Henderson is a true master at his craft—a phenomenal caster, angler, fly tier, photographer, and teacher—making him one of the most sought-after fly-fishing guides in Colorado.

According to Henderson, "Sculpins are abundant on the Yampa River and they represent a large protein source for opportunistic trout, which makes a sculpin imitation a great choice for any streamer enthusiast. When designing a pattern to imitate a sculpin, you must carefully choose the materials, mimic the correct profile, and understand how to fish it. Incorporating all of these facets into the design led to the creation of my Bunny Sculpin."

Steve Henderson's Bunny Sculpin is a pattern that I highly recommend. Certain watersheds like the Yampa River near Steamboat Springs are known for their robust population of sculpins. Trout waste little time ambushing a sculpin because they provide a huge meal for an opportunistic trout.

Choosing the proper fly-tying materials can make or break your success with a streamer. The most important attribute to any baitfish imitation is that it must look alive. "Fur on a hide, like the rabbit strips I use in my Bunny Sculpin, provides incredible wiggling and undulating movement for this pattern. This remains true whether it's fished with a fast stripping action or a very slow retrieve. Some fly-tying materials are stiff and do not perform well in the water. Using a bunny strip on this pattern makes it look 'alive,' with little input needed from the angler."

It's hard to go wrong with the tried-and-true size, shape, and color formula when designing a trout fly. "Sculpins have large heads, and their body tapers back to their tail. In order to imitate this profile, a bunny strip is used for the back of the fly and palmered to form a head. An additional bunny strip is added to form pectoral fins, which increases the head profile even further. The larger head in comparison to the body also helps create increased motion on the tail as it moves in the current. Sculpins are naturally camouflaged to blend in with the streambed. Throughout the calendar year, a

Steve Henderson enticed this Yampa River rainbow to eat one of his black Bunny Sculpins. Henderson will quickly make a believer out of you that you can catch trout year-round with streamers—even during the dead of winter.

river can change its streambed color from a springtime sandy-tan to a fall mossy-olive."

Henderson goes on to explain that there are numerous color variations that can be tied, but the most common color combinations that he uses are natural grizzly/cream, olive variant/cream, brown/ginger, black, and rust with yellow pectoral fins. He believes that each color has a time and place. Henderson offers this advice with regard to choosing a specific color and the tactics he uses. "I begin by trying to match the streambed with a color scheme in my fly box. The Bunny Sculpin is tied with lead eyes and an upturned hook. Sculpins are bottom dwellers that spend their lives moving over and around rocks primarily in the rivers' riffles. The Bunny Sculpin should be fished close to the substrate, and whenever possible try to occasionally bounce it along the bottom. Tying the Bunny Sculpin with an upturned hook and lead eyes allows it to be fished close to the bottom where sculpins reside with fewer chances of hanging up."

Henderson recommends fishing this pattern year-round, regardless of the conditions. "I fish this pattern year-round in both high and low water. During higher flow regimes, a sinking or sink tip line is useful to get the fly close to bottom. A floating line is appropriate for most late summer, fall, and winter months. When walk-wading I primarily like to fish this pattern with a slow across-and-downstream swing with a few gentle strips to bump the fly along the substrate. I consider the presentation complete once the fly line becomes taught and straightens below me. I repeat this presentation, walking downstream a few steps before each new cast. When I'm fishing from a drift boat, I typically cast the fly toward the stream bank and use the conventional swing and strip approach. The important thing to remember is to keep positive tension on the fly in order to feel the take."

Caddis Emerger

(Tied by Son Tao)

- **Hook:** #10–#16 Hanak H 300 BL
- **Wing:** Elk hair
- **Flash:** Pearlescent Krystal flash
- **Body:** Stripped peacock quill over green holographic tinsel coated with UV resin
- **Hackle:** Whiting Farms ginger variant rooster

If you ask any of the top industry professionals why they tie flies, chances are good you will get several different answers. For many, fly tying keeps them connected to the sport when they cannot get to the stream, while others tie flies out of necessity to keep their guide boxes full, commercial tiers make a living or subsidize their income tying flies, and yet others enjoy the craft because it unleashes their creativity and helps them solve a problem. Several people I know tie flies for therapeutic reasons to help clear their minds from the day-to-day stresses in life. I can honestly say that I tie flies for all of these reasons.

Over my tenure as a professional guide, I have met some talented individuals that I am proud to call my friends. Son Tao is one of those gifted tiers that takes fly tying to the next level. From tiny midges to the most difficult dry flies and streamers, Tao ties them all, striving for perfection with each wrap of thread.

Tao was born in southern Vietnam in 1974. His family fled to Malaysia as political refugees when he was 6 years old. They lived

Son Tao is a perfectionist when it comes to tying flies. Whether he is tying a dry fly, nymph, or a big, beefy streamer, each wrap of thread has a purpose. Tao's Caddis Emerger is a great option for anglers who enjoy fishing an evening caddis hatch. Tao's Caddis Emerger can be dead-drifted or skated to imitate egg-laying adults.

in a refugee camp for a year and a half and were denied political asylum by every country except the United States. In 1980 Tao arrived in the United States and settled in Lancaster County, Pennsylvania.

Tao worked as an engineer for a few years after college until September 11, 2001. After the tragic events of 9/11, he enlisted in the US Army as a way to pay back the United States for accepting his family as immigrants and for the freedom they enjoy. Tao is currently an active-duty first sergeant in the US Army. He has served our nation for 19 years and deployed numerous times all over the world as an infantryman.

Tao began tying flies a few years ago to help deal with anxiety from years of deployments to war zones. Combat stress, loss of soldiers, and suffering some traumatic injuries eventually led to sleepless nights, alcohol dependency, and depression. Fly fishing became a powerful healing tool that quickly became a passion.

If you spend any time with Tao, it won't take you long to figure out that he is a superb angler and fly tier. After one year of tying, Tao won the Project Healing Waters Fly Fishing National Fly Tying competition. He quickly earned a reputation as a perfectionist and graciously shares his photography, tying tutorials, and videos on a number of social media platforms.

Currently, Tao is stationed in Colorado and pursues trout all over the Centennial State. He has a fondness for the South Platte River and can typically be seen every weekend at Deckers, the Dream Stream, Eleven Mile Canyon, or Cheesman Canyon. He also enjoys fishing high mountain lakes and small streams to escape the crowds.

According to Tao, he designed his Caddis Emerger as an attractor to entice trout that are feeding opportunistically. Tao fishes this pattern a variety of ways—on the dead drift, skated, or fished in conjunction with a dropper. "I created this fly as a searching pattern for the summer evening caddis hatches. I typically fish it with either a caddis pupa or midge dropper. It's a versatile pattern that can easily be tied in a variety of sizes and colors to mimic caddis that emerge in local waters. The peacock quill provides a natural-looking segmentation that is punctuated with UV resin. The holographic tinsel and midge Krystal Flash helps mimic the gas bubble effect that occurs when caddis emerge. The elk hair wing and rooster hackle provide great visibility and buoyance." Tao finds that if he ties his Caddis Emerger with red holographic tinsel (instead of the quill body), it's extremely effective for brook and cutthroat trout in the smaller mountain streams.

Tao encourages anglers to think outside the box and don't be afraid to skitter or twitch this pattern, especially in pocket water. "This pattern works especially well right before dusk, precisely when you'll find egg-laying caddis abundant near the water's surface." If you're using a caddis pupa as a dropper, it never hurts to allow it to swing in the current, as the uplifting action routinely entices a "grab" during the evening hours.

Son Tao caught this chunky rainbow trout on his Caddis Emerger during an evening caddis emergence on the South Platte River below Spinney Dam. One advantage to this pattern is that it is easy to see—even in the harsh evening glare. SON TAO

CDC Callibaetis Nymph

(Tied by Herman deGala)

- **Hook:** #14–#16 Tiemco 2302
- **Bead:** Gold 2.0 mm
- **Tail:** Rust ostrich herl
- **Abdomen:** Rust ostrich herl and Rust D-Rib (Small)
- **Wing case:** Mottled Brown Medallion Sheeting, coated with Loon UV resin
- **Legs:** Rust CDC

Colorado residents are blessed with some phenomenal lake fishing. Whether you're fishing in the metro area, South Park, or one of the state's legendary alpine lakes, there are dozens of stillwater options to choose from. Stillwater impoundments are especially important during the high-water season (spring runoff), when many of our rivers and streams are blown out and difficult to fish.

Early summer brings lake enthusiasts reliable hatches of *Callibaetis* mayflies, with their emergences often peaking during the height of spring runoff. *Callibaetis* mayflies are multibrooded, meaning they have two or three generations per season, with the first mayflies emerging in late May or early June. Their life cycle is approximately six weeks from egg to a sexually mature adult. Subsequent generations continue to hatch through the early part of September. Similar to their moving water cousins (*Baetis*), each succeeding brood is smaller than the previous generation, requiring anglers to adjust their fly sizes (downsizing them) as the season progresses.

Callibaetis typically begin hatching around 10 a.m. and continue for a couple hours. The

The importance of having a thorough selection of Callibaetis *nymphs cannot be overemphasized. Herman deGala's CDC Callibaetis Nymph is one you should definitely consider carrying in your fly box. DeGala's design incorporates the use of fluffy materials (ostrich herl and CDC) because it simulates life under a wide range of conditions.*

best hatches occur when skies are overcast or during inclement weather. Rain showers can produce epic hatches, as the high humidity stalls the development of the emerging duns, keeping them on the water longer, in comparison to bright and sunny days. To successfully match the hatch, you'll need to have a pattern that imitates the nymph and, of course, a variety of dry flies to imitate the dun and spinner.

Herman deGala's CDC Callibaetis Nymph is a great imposter for the emerging nymph. If you've seen any of deGala's patterns, they are true works of art. Their realistic appearance mimics the natural in almost every way. "By education, I am a designer. We are taught a methodology for solving design problems, be it a large community development or something as small as an appliance. I approach designing flies in a similar way. I have fished several other patterns that were meant to mimic the behavior of a *Callibaetis* nymph—they all worked—but there seemed to be something missing. The flies didn't quite behave in the manner that I felt they should. So I designed a pattern that I truly believe impersonates a *Callibaetis* nymph. I started

Stillwater aficionados mark the Callibaetis *hatch in their calendars because it provides some of the best fishing opportunities of the year. Fish like this Antero Reservoir rainbow are commonly fooled with a Callibaetis nymph stripped over a weed bed.* LANDON MAYER

with a long hook shank so that the thickness of the fly would be in proportion to its length. Next, I wanted to make sure there was enough of a gape to ensure a good hookup after the materials were wrapped around the shank. I also needed a stout hook, because the strikes are often aggressive with *Callibaetis* nymphs, including the reaction from the fish once it knows it's been fooled. For this reason, I went with a Tiemco 2302 versus the 200R, which provided me with the best of both worlds."

Prior to emergence, *Callibaetis* nymphs swim upward, oftentimes becoming fidgety as they move up and down in the water column. Trapped gases help the nymphs ascend to the water's surface, where emergence occurs. Trout are always looking for these rising and falling nymphs prior to the hatch. Callibaetis nymphs should be fished with tiny strips so that they "rise and fall" over a weed bed, the lifelike movement that triggers a strike. Many anglers like to fish their Callibaetis nymphs off a strike indicator, with a simple jigging action as they kick their fins in their pontoon boat to move over the weed beds.

"The materials I use in my Callibaetis nymph have to project movement along the weed beds even when the fly is static in between strips. The CDC provides that movement. I felt my Callibaetis needed a touch of weight, so I added a bead, which helped put its head down, eliciting a quick strike before it scooted away."

If you're looking for a reliable Callibaetis emerger, try using a Quigley Cripple. There are several imitations that work well for the duns and spinners, starting with something as simple as a size 14 Parachute Adams. Comparadun patterns, and a wide array of Callibaetis Parachutes, are equally effective.

Cinnamon Spinner

(Tied by Mike Kruise)

- **Hook:** #16–#22 Tiemco 100
- **Thread:** Rusty-brown 8/0 Veevus
- **Tail:** Light-dun mayfly tails
- **Body:** Dave Whitlock's Red Fox Squirrel dubbing blended with a small amount of cinnamon High and Dry dubbing with a stand of white organza wrapped on the body
- **Wing:** Natural CDC with a few rust-brown Z-Lon fibers

Mike Kruise grew up fishing northern Colorado's local waters—the St. Vrain, Big Thompson, Cache la Poudre, and the lakes and streams of Rocky Mountain National Park. Kruise's lifelong passion for fly fishing and tying flies led him to join forces with his friend Scott Bley to launch Laughing Grizzly Fly Shop in Longmont, Colorado, in May of 2007. The team of professionals at Laughing Grizzly Fly Shop specialize in fooling trout on many of the nearby streams in and around Rocky Mountain National Park. Kruise is also the co-author with Steve Schweitzer of *A Fly*

Fishing Guide to Indian Peaks Wilderness Area. The Indian Peaks Wilderness Area is just south of Rocky Mountain National Park, nestled between the James Peaks Wilderness on the south and small sections of the "park" on the north, straddling the Continental Divide.

When Kruise is not working in the fly shop, tying flies, or guiding on his home waters, you'll find him spending some time on some of the state's other renowned trout streams like the Frying Pan, Roaring Fork, Crystal, South Platte, or Tarryall Creek. "If you spend any length of time in the Roaring Fork Valley, it

Mike Kruise's Cinnamon Spinner is a pattern that imitates the final stage of a mayfly's development. Pale morning duns, red quills, and tiny blue-winged olives turn a rust color when they transform from a dun into a spinner.

won't take you long to figure out you'll need a reliable rusty spinner pattern. A rusty or cinnamon-colored spinner pattern is a classic dry fly that every angler should carry in their fly box."

Several varieties of mayflies (pale morning duns, red quills, and blue-winged olives) turn a rusty color when they transform from a dun into a spinner. "The Cinnamon Spinner was born out of necessity when a buddy of mine and I were on a three-day trip to the Frying Pan River. The dry-fly fishing was excellent on our first afternoon, but I didn't have the exact fly the trout were looking for. I did seine a few of the rusty spinners and carefully studied them. That evening I tied up a few variations of a rusty spinner in our hotel room to be used the following day."

Kruise tied a variety of spinner patterns, some with dubbed bodies and others with turkey biots. "For some reason, the spinners I tied with cinnamon dubbing and natural CDC and a few fibers of rust-brown Z-Lon for the wings were the best producers. The design is quite simple actually. The tail is composed of light-dun mayfly tails, which are approximately two shank lengths long. The body is a mixture of Dave Whitlock's Red Fox Squirrel dubbing blended with a hint of cinnamon High and Dry dubbing. I use a strand of white organza to simulate the ribbing to add a bit of sheen to the abdomen. The wing is made of natural CDC and a few fibers of rust-brown Z-Lon."

The following week Kruise tried his Cinnamon Spinner closer to home in Wild Basin. "The brookies and browns loved it up there; I was getting strikes in just about every hole. Since then, I have used the Cinnamon Spinner in every body of water that I have fished in the Indian Peaks Wilderness Area. Needless to say, it has become one of my go-to dry flies, and one of my top guide flies in Rocky Mountain National Park."

Kruise recommends fishing his Cinnamon Spinner with a 12-foot leader terminating in 6X tippet. It's important to use dry-fly crystals on this pattern, because conventional paste floatants ruin the fluffy CDC wing and cause it to sink. In Rocky Mountain National Park, Kruise fishes his Cinnamon Spinner as a single dry fly because the trout are easily spooked with the gin clear water. "Long cast with a delicate touch are mandatory for success. One poor cast and the game is over! I like to sneak up from behind the trout and keep my false casting to a minimum. You don't want the trout to see your fly line, so I recommend using a 12-foot leader with 18 to 24 inches of 6X tippet." If you do approach a rising trout from the side, make sure you use a reach mend. "A reach mend is nothing more than adjusting your fly line and leader (tippet) in the air so that fly is the first thing the trout sees. It's a deadly tactic once you master it."

A Cinnamon Spinner is one of Mike Kruise's favorite flies in Rocky Mountain National Park. It is also one of his go-to dry flies for the nearby Indian Peaks Wilderness Area. Kruise recommends tying the Cinnamon Spinner in sizes 16 to 22 to be prepared to imitate spinner falls of pale morning duns, red quills, and blue-winged olives.

Colorado Crystal Beetle

(Tied by Rich Pilatzke)

- **Hook:** #10–#18 Tiemco 100
- **Thread:** Black 6/0 Uni-Thread
- **Underbody:** Hareline Speckled Chenille lime/black
- **Overbody:** 2 mm black craft foam
- **Legs:** Hareline Black Krystal Flash
- **Indicator:** ⅛" yellow Evazote foam

You would be hard-pressed to strike up a conversation about Colorado's still waters without Richard Pilatzke's name coming up in the discussion. Pilatzke is hands down one of the most respected lake anglers in Colorado, not to mention a phenomenal fly tier. The Colorado Crystal Beetle has been a staple for Pilatzke over the past 30 years. Like many proven patterns, the Colorado Crystal Beetle went through a series of changes and rigorous field testing to improve the final product.

According to Pilatzke, "The Colorado Crystal Beetle began in its embryonic form with the first fly-tying foam that I was able to find in the late 1980s. I remember watching a guide from Blue Ribbon Flies in West Yellowstone, Montana, tying the Blue Ribbon Beetle at the FFF Fly Fishing Museum. It was a simple black foam beetle tied with Traun River

Rich Pilatzke's Colorado Crystal Beetle is a proven pattern that stillwater enthusiasts have come to depend on for over 30 years. It can be fished as a single dry fly or used in combination with a Chironomid, Callibaetis nymph, or scud dropper. The Colorado Crystal Beetle is equally effective on moving water, as opportunistic trout rarely refuse the chance to capitalize on an effortless meal, especially on the downwind side of the stream bank, where terrestrials frequently fall into the river.

foam, a product from Austria. I was fascinated with tying and fishing terrestrials, so I decided I was going to tie a few up. It didn't take me long to figure out that an all-black beetle or ant was almost impossible to see on the water. That's when I started experimenting with indicators to make the beetle more visible. I was fishing at Quincy Reservoir at the time and I tried using different Christmas-wrapping yarns in red, orange, green, and yellow, tied in over the eye of the hook. I soon discovered ⅛-inch yellow Evazote foam that was available at some local fly shops and switched to using that for the indicator. That quickly took care of that problem, enabling me to see my black beetle at a considerable distance."

The next progression occurred when Pilatzke noticed that the underside of many beetles had a metallic green color with a lot of iridescence. "I found a green-and-black chenille in a local fly shop and used it for the underbody of my beetle. I later sourced the chenille and purchased ten skeins from the Danville Chenille Company in Danville, New Hampshire. I've tied upwards of 2,000 dozen

Whether you're fishing one of your favorite stillwater impoundments or spending the day on a small, meandering meadow stream in South Park, the Colorado Crystal Beetle is a great searching pattern. On moving water the Colorado Crystal Beetle is deadly fished tight to a grassy bank.

Colorado Crystal Beetles and still have a couple skeins left."

Pilatzke originally used moose body hair for the legs but has since replaced it with black Krystal Flash. "The moose hair was brittle, and the legs fell apart. Swapping the moose with black Krystal Flash was an easy fix."

Pilatzke recommends using the Colorado Crystal Beetle for a searching pattern on still waters. "The Colorado Crystal Beetle is by far the single-most productive fly that I have fished in Colorado, catching thousands of trout, bass, bluegills, and crappie." Pilatzke recommends casting a beetle out on the water and letting it sit for a few seconds, then twitching it a couple times. If nothing happens, pick it up and recast. "I don't let my flies sit for long—I like to cover a lot of water because I believe if a trout sees the fly in their window of vision, they'll take it."

Don't rule out using a Colorado Crystal Beetle with a dropper below it. Suspending a size 12 Chironomid, size 16 Callibaetis nymph, or size 14 scud below it can be deadly, especially if there is a little chop on the water. The wavelike action causes a jigging action that often attracts nearby trout.

Beetles are equally effective on moving water, especially small, meandering meadow streams. Several streams in South Park are great places to fish with beetles. When the breeze picks up in the afternoon, target the downwind banks, because opportunistic trout are always looking for an easy meal. Terrestrials provide trout with more bang for the buck, so they don't waste any time feeding on them once they hit the water. Strange as it might sound, the Colorado Crystal Beetle is a good midge-cluster imitation. It's easy to see under a wide range of conditions, but, more important, the flashy chenille underbody seems to portray the movement of midges crawling on top of one another when they are clustered up.

- **Hook:** #8 Tiemco 5262
- **Thread:** Danville tan 3/0 monocord
- **Tail:** Yellow over tan Woolly Bugger Marabou
- **Body hackle:** Light ginger Hebert Hen saddle
- **Body:** Light-yellow UV Ice Dubbing
- **Connection:** 30-pound test SpiderWire
- **Articulation beads:** 2 brown pearl CFB 4 mm Baby Beads
- **Eyes:** Yellow small double pupil lead eyes
- **Front body:** Light-yellow UV Ice Dub
- **Legs:** Black/gold Chrome Sili Legs
- **Collar:** Shrimp Polar Fiber
- **Head:** Shrimp Polar Fiber spun in a dubbing loop, wrapped and trimmed to shape
- **Coloring:** Jasmine and sepia Prismacolor Markers

Craven's Baby Gonga

(Tied by Charlie Craven)

Charlie Craven is one of the most innovative fly tiers of our time. From tiny midge imitations to articulated streamers and everything in between, Craven is a true master when it comes to designing flies. The driving force behind Craven's innovation is to design flies that are realistic, breathe life, float better, sink quicker, and remain durable even after they have been fished hard and pushed to the brink.

If you're a die-hard streamer enthusiast, it won't take you long to figure out why the Baby Gonga is Craven's favorite streamer. It's interesting to pick Craven's brain from time to time and listen to what he has to say. "The Baby Gonga came about a few years after the full-sized Double Gonga was introduced. I was driving home from a float trip thinking about what made the fish so attracted to articulated flies and wondered if it was the sheer size of the bigger patterns or if it really was the broken-back wiggle that enticed an aggressive grab. I hatched the idea to tie a Gonga in a baby size, about half as big as the original but with an articulation point in the middle to help answer the question. I got to

Casting one of Charlie Craven's Baby Gongas from a drift boat or inflatable raft is about as good as it gets. The moment leading up to the "grab" is what keeps us entertained for hours in search of the trout of a lifetime.

fish it the following week and had my answer. The Baby Gonga has all the allure of its bigger brother but sinks better, is far easier to cast, is an easy, nonintimidating bite, and with its smaller hooks, it really digs in for a good purchase when fish eat it."

Craven recommends tying his Baby Gonga in black, olive, rainbow, rust, tan/yellow (baby brown trout color), and gray. "I tie the Baby Gonga in one size, two Tiemco 5262 size 8 hooks tethered together with SpiderWire and a couple of beads, though I have recently been playing with some short-shank stinger hooks with the same shank length but a slightly wider hook gap, but the results are still out on that version. I typically start with the tan version on any given day as it is the easiest to see in the water and I like to watch it all happen whenever I can. If that color isn't turning heads, I'll go straight to black and then work my way through the other colors in no particular order from there. I confess, I can usually catch them

Hunter Dorsey is one of many anglers who have come to appreciate Charlie Craven's innovative fly patterns. This large rainbow was fooled with one of Craven's tan-and-yellow Baby Gongas.

on whatever variation I want to throw, so the color of the day is really just up to my mood."

The most effective method to fish a Baby Gonga is with a traditional downstream presentation, using the classic strip-and-swing technique. Cast your Baby Gonga as tight to the stream bank as possible, then lower your rod tip and begin stripping the fly. Undercut banks are great locations to find massive trout, so always be looking for them. It's important to vary your retrieve—sometimes a slow strip entices a strike, while other times a faster presentation works better. The best advice I can give you is to cover as much water as possible, and be methodical, as repetitive casting in the same area has a diminishing return. Fishing a streamer from a drift boat or inflatable raft gives an angler the upper hand because it allows them to cover several miles of water in a day.

Streamer fishing is a fun and relaxing way to hunt for large fish—but make no mistake about it: It's hard work! In most cases the rewards are worth the effort, however, because large fish tend to be opportunistic feeders and willing to chase big flies, especially realistic streamer patterns that mimic baitfish with lifelike movements.

Craven offers this bit of advice: "I like to fish the Baby Gonga on a floating line with a 9-foot 0X leader with a 0X fluorocarbon tippet, preferably from a drifting boat or raft. I do sometimes employ a short sink tip line as well, but with a much shorter leader to allow the tip to pull the fly more horizontally through the water. As I mentioned, I am a voyeur and like to watch the show, so I am more apt to fish the floating line with the fly up in the water column where I can see it well, but that's just me."

- **Hook:** #12–#16 Tiemco 100
- **Thread:** Tan 70 denier UTC
- **Body:** Amber Australian opossum
- **Palmer hackle:** Whiting Farms Cree rooster cape or saddle
- **Rib:** Copper UTC wire (extra small) for hackle reinforcement
- **Underwing:** Natural dun CDC feather tied flat
- **Overwing:** Whiting Farms golden-speckled badger Coq de Leon stacked rooster barbules
- **Collar hackle:** Whiting Farms brown rooster

Fast Water Caddis

(Tied by Michael Gula)

Colorado is home to some of the best free-stone streams in the western United States. Unregulated trout streams can be challenging at times because they are completely dependent on Mother Nature's snowfields and rainfall, but when conditions are right—stable flows, steady water temperatures, and consistent hatches—they can provide some exceptional fishing.

Freestone streams are known for their classic riffles, runs, pool tailouts, pronounced mid-channel shelves, and fabulous pocket water. Free-flowing streams have a tendency to be big and fast in comparison to smooth-flowing tailwaters, so having a durable, heavily hack-led dry fly that floats well and is easy to see can make or break your success.

Michael Gula's Fast Water Caddis is a pattern that I would highly recommend for western freestones and some of the state's larger tailwaters. Whether you're trying to match the hatch in April or May (Mother's Day caddis hatch) or prospecting for opportunistic trout during the summer months, its bombproof construction allows it to float on the choppiest of currents.

"I developed my Fast Water Caddis in the early 2000s to satisfy a searching-type pattern

The Fast Water Caddis, as the name implies, was designed to withstand the heaviest of currents and not sink. Michael Gula's design is perfect for a searching pattern on western freestone streams where heavy concentrations of caddis are found. Gula ties his Fast Water Caddis in three different colors to imitate a variety of species.

Michael Gula's Fast Water Caddis, as the name implies, floats exceptionally well on choppy currents. Its heavily hackled design makes it a great candidate for a searching pattern in riffles, runs, and pocket water. Don't be afraid to skitter the Fast Water Caddis from time to time, as this strategy often produces an aggressive strike!

when caddis are buzzing around the stream. I wanted a fly that was light and easy to cast—and, most important, floated well. I created light, medium (pictured), and dark versions to cover the myriad caddis species found on western rivers." Gula tweaks the color of the Australian Opossum and the hackle (abdomen and collar) to lighten or darken his caddis imitations.

"I'm partial to using natural materials whenever possible, although I do occasionally integrate synthetics when I feel the fly design merits their use. I guess I'm old-school," Gula said. Old-school or not, Gula, a Whiting Farms Pro Team member, is extremely talented when it comes to designing and tying dry flies. "Patterns like the Elk Hair Caddis and Stimulator are very effective flies and I use them often. However, I wanted to come up with a series of caddisflies that incorporated a bit of translucency into the design, with the ability for light

to pass through them. Integrating a palmer hackle, CDC underwing, and stacked CDL barbs satisfied that. The stiffness of the barbs, their length, and the subtle speckling within colors affords the fly tier quite a range of possibilities. I wanted to utilize those feathers for something other than dry-fly tailing material. The CDL stacked barb overwing married with the CDC underwing created the profile I was looking for."

Gula offers this suggestion with regard to tying the overwing. He advises taking four sections of CDL barbs about the width of an index finger and stripping them from the rachis (stem). The curled butt section should be clipped off and placed in a hair stacker, tips down to even them up. Then remove the CDL barbs from the stacker and tie them on top of the CDC underwing.

Caddis imitations can be dead-drifted or skated depending on what you are trying to accomplish. Newly hatched caddis sit on the water prior to taking flight, but egg layers bounce up and down near the water's surface as they try to lay their eggs. If you're not getting strikes with a dead-drifted caddis, try skating it.

Gula recommends fishing a two-fly tandem rig, one light caddis and one dark caddis, or one medium and one dark, and so on, to imitate multiple species of caddis on the water. "When prospecting with caddis patterns, I use a tandem rig to increase my odds. I cover the water quickly with a cast or two into each desired location before moving on. The materials I use in the Fast Water Caddis allow it to float well in pocket water, riffles, and runs. One or two false casts is all that is necessary to dry the caddis off and get them back on the water." It's a good idea to put the light-colored caddis (locator fly) in front of the darker version to help see it. If you see a rise anywhere near your locator fly, assume a fish took the darker caddis and set the hook.

Foam Green Drake

(Tied by Ben Furimsky)

- **Hook:** #10–#12 Tiemco 100
- **Thread:** 6/0 rusty-brown Uni-Thread
- **Tail:** Black calf-tail hair
- **Body:** Olive Evazote foam
- **Hackle:** Dun and olive dyed grizzly rooster
- **Thorax:** Peacock herl
- **Wing:** Dun poly

Every summer anglers anxiously await the arrival of the fabled green drake hatch in Colorado. The hatch typically begins in late June and continues through the first part of August, providing anglers with some of the best dry-fly fishing of the summer season.

On western trout streams the green drake is the largest mayfly, measuring nearly 1 inch in length. When you see a green drake on the water, they look like a battleship in comparison to pale morning duns, Tricos, red quills, and blue-winged olives. Colorado's hatches are a combination of two different species:

Drunella grandis and *Drunella doddsii*. The physical appearance of the duns is similar, with the exception of the *Drunella doddsii* being slightly smaller in size. It's not uncommon for both species to live in the same stream, so I recommend filling your fly box with an assortment of green drake imitations in sizes 10 to 14 to cover your bases.

Green drakes thrive in streams with cobbled substrates and prefer moderate to fast-paced currents. The "drake hatch" is found on several streams in Colorado—both freestones and tailwaters—which is a huge advantage for

Green drake hatches in Colorado produce some epic dry-fly fishing during the summer months. Being in the right place at the right time with a proven pattern like Ben Furimsky's Foam Green Drake stacks the odds in your favor for success. Furimsky's Foam Green Drake is perfect for choppy western waters because it is easy to see and floats extremely well.

anglers, especially during the onset of spring runoff, when unregulated streams can become unpredictable. As a general rule, anglers can find reliable green drake hatches on the Gunnison, East, Roaring Fork, Frying Pan, Eagle, Yampa, Blue, and South Platte Rivers. The hatches begin in lower elevations first, then gradually move up the watershed as the water temperatures rise. Being in the right place at the right time is critical for success, so it never hurts to check with local authorities to pinpoint the exact location of the hatch.

Living in Crested Butte, Furimsky is blessed with the opportunity to partake in some phenomenal dry-fly fishing on the East, Gunnison, and Taylor Rivers, as well as many of the area's smaller creeks. "My Foam Drake was designed to specifically imitate the western green drake. I noticed that many of the traditional patterns didn't accurately match the hatch. The colors were off, or they were made as an extended body, but the wing and hackle were not 'extended.' Careful observation of green drakes leads me to believe that most imitations are not proportionally correct. The natural's wing is longer than the body, the tails are short and stubby, and the body is fat with heavy segments," says Furimsky.

Furimsky's Foam Green Drake is a thing of beauty. He uses gray Evazote foam for a segmented body and black calf tail for the tail. The tail is tied short, about one-third of shank length long. The foam is soft and has a sheen that looks similar to a newly hatched dun. The extended body is slightly curved and the segments are punctuated with brown thread. To create a tapered abdomen, Furimsky adjusts the thread tension (tighter toward the tail) and spacing of the segments (slightly larger toward the thorax) as he progresses forward on the abdomen.

The next step is developing the thorax. "I add peacock herl, overlaid by an olive grizzly rooster hackle to keep the flies' profile correct, and a dun-colored McFlylon wing for the ease of tying and the proper silhouette of the wing. Trimming the bottom of the hackle helps keep the fly balanced while being slightly oversized for the hook it is tied on. The Foam Drake floats incredibly well, especially in the fast water where the greatest populations of green drakes are found."

Furimsky often fishes his Foam Drake with a PMD nymph dropper because the two hatches typically coincide. The PMDs typically come off a little earlier in the day (10:30 a.m. to 12:30 p.m.), then the green drakes follow, starting around 1 p.m. "If the fish are feeding on the Foam Green Drake consistently, I snip off the dropper and focus on the dry-fly fishing. The Foam Drake typically brings up some large fish with exciting takes. I've found that a drag-free drift is important. I usually fish a 3X leader (tippet) to prevent leader twist with a large fly. The larger-diameter tippet also assists in accurate cast with a good turnover. If you truly feel that 3X is causing refusals, drop to 4X, but I never go lower than that."

Craig Davis scoops up a brown trout that he caught on a size 12 Furimsky's Foam Green Drake on the Taylor River several miles above Almont. The green drake hatch typically begins in mid- to late July and extends into the first week of August.

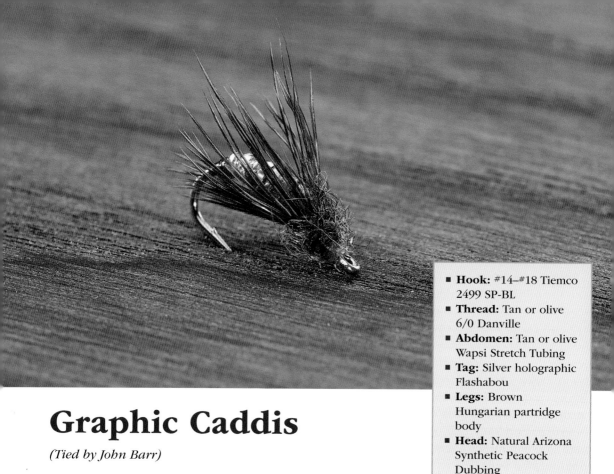

Graphic Caddis

(Tied by John Barr)

- **Hook:** #14–#18 Tiemco 2499 SP-BL
- **Thread:** Tan or olive 6/0 Danville
- **Abdomen:** Tan or olive Wapsi Stretch Tubing
- **Tag:** Silver holographic Flashabou
- **Legs:** Brown Hungarian partridge body
- **Head:** Natural Arizona Synthetic Peacock Dubbing

John Barr's Graphic Caddis is a must-have during the height of a caddis hatch, when trout are feeding voraciously on pupae. Colorado is known for its epic caddis hatches that occur on many of the state's freestone streams. Caddis hatches aren't shabby on several of Colorado's tailwaters either, so anglers should be prepared to imitate this important food source on most of the streams in Colorado.

Caddis hatches begin in late April and continue through the latter part of the summer, with sporadic emergences occurring well into the autumn months. If you have experienced a dense caddis hatch, then you know exactly what I am talking about—it's one of the most amazing sights you'll see on a trout stream. Watching a group of suspended trout sweep back and forth gobbling caddis pupae is about as good as it gets.

In *Barr Flies* Barr explains the importance of caddis pupae. "Wherever there are caddis larvae, there are caddis pupae. Caddis will hatch spring through fall, so trout get accustomed to seeing the pupae and readily accept them as a tasty treat, whether caddis are hatching or not. After eight or nine months, the caddis

John Barr's Graphic Caddis is a good option when you see trout sweeping back and forth feeding on caddis pupae. Barr's Graphic Caddis can be fished in a tandem nymphing rig or underneath a dry fly as a dropper. Don't be afraid to let this fly swing in the current, because it typically produces an aggressive take when the leader tightens and the fly rises in the water column.

larvae pupate for about a month. Throughout that month, they gradually transform into fully mature pupae, ready to hatch into adults. While they are pupating, they are hidden from trout and are not available as a food source. Once they are mature and get ready to emerge, they become an extremely important food source."

Barr ties the Graphic Caddis in two different color schemes: tan (actually looks gray) and olive. According to Barr, "The name Graphic Caddis comes from the use of the silver holographic Flashabou under the stretch tubing body. The Flashabou gives the illusion of the silvery air bubble that accompanies a pupa as it ascends in the water column." The stretch tubing produces a beautiful, slightly tapered body with realistic segmentation. For the legs, Barr uses brown Hungarian partridge, and for the wing pads (fluffy collar in front of the wing), the original recipe suggests using gray ostrich herl. Many of Barr's patterns continue to evolve over time. "In recent years I have used dubbing instead of ostrich herl to simulate the wing pads."

Sadie Olsen and the author admire a beautiful rainbow that she caught on a tan Barr's Graphic Caddis. It's not uncommon to see sporadic caddis hatches in Cheesman Canyon until mid-October, particularly when the reservoir turns over and the water temperatures rise into the mid-50s Fahrenheit. The increase in water temperature triggers caddis hatches that add a lot of excitement during the onset of the autumn season. BRENT TAYLOR

In a casual conversation with Barr, he offered this great advice: "The Graphic Caddis has been my go-to pupa pattern for years. It's not an exact science, but if the adult caddis hatching are dark, I like to use an olive pupa, and to the contrary, if the adults are light, I use a tan imitation." I routinely find myself covering my bases and fishing with one of each color during the height of a caddis hatch.

Barr recommends fishing his Graphic Caddis a number of ways. He routinely swings the Graphic Caddis into a bulging or splashy-type rise form. He'll cast 6 to 8 feet above the trout, then raise the rod tip so that the leader becomes taut, then allows the fly to lift in front of the trout's head. This is a technique that was mastered by Jim Leisenring many decades ago called the Leisenring Lift. "I also use the Graphic Caddis as a dropper under an adult during a caddis hatch or include it as part of my Hopper-Copper-Dropper technique."

Don't rule out fishing the Graphic Caddis with a conventional nymphing rig either. Since the Graphic Caddis is a pupa, it should be fished as the second or third fly in a tandem nymphing rig so that it rides higher in the current in comparison to the fly closest to the weight. I typically fish the Graphic Caddis off a caddis larva, then trail a Graphic Caddis below it. As a general rule, I space them out about 12 inches apart. It is important to fish the Graphic Caddis mid-column, precisely where you'll find heavy concentrations of pupae rising toward the surface to emerge. Too much weight is as problematic as not enough when you are targeting suspended trout. I recommend using a yarn strike indicator that is easily adjustable to keep your flies in the correct feeding zone.

Barr recommends stocking your fly boxes with both tan and olive Graphic Caddis in sizes 14 to 18. He also admits it's not a bad idea to carry a few size 20s to imitate micro caddis that are found in some drainages.

- **Hook:** #8–#10 Tiemco 5263
- **Thread:** Dark-brown UTC 70 denier
- **Weight:** .020 lead-free wire
- **Underbody:** UTC Opal Mirage tinsel (large)
- **Abdomen:** Light-brown Squirmy Worm material
- **Shellback:** Brown Hareline scud back
- **Ribbing:** Dark-brown UTC wire (Brassie)
- **Head finish:** Fulling Mill glass UV resin

Gummy Crane

(Tied by Joe Shafer)

My success with crane-fly larvae was hit-or-miss until I started using Joe Shafer's Gummy Crane. Many of my early attempts to tie crane-fly larvae with latex, rawhide, rubber bands, and dubbed fur bodies were disappointing at best. Having faith and confidence in your fly stacks the odds in your favor when it comes to fooling trout. If you're skeptical about your flies, you typically don't fish them as hard as you do with a proven producer. Shafer's Gummy Crane has instilled that confidence in crane-fly larvae so much so that it is one of my go-to attractors in a tandem nymphing rig.

Shafer designed his Gummy Crane to fill an important void in his fly box. "If you flip over a rock or seine in one of your favorite trout streams, chances are good you'll find a bunch of crane flies. Several years ago I did some research on crane-fly larvae and found out there are over 500 species in North America. My research, streamside observation, and seine samples, led me to develop a pattern to mimic a crane-fly larva."

Opportunistic trout waste no time eating Joe Shafer's Gummy Crane. Shafer's Gummy Crane went through rigorous field testing and a series of modifications before he was happy with it. The end result is a super-realistic crane-fly larva that is soft and squishy like the naturals, so trout chew on it instead of rejecting it. The Gummy Crane has no doubt become a local favorite for both guides and anglers alike.

Shafer carefully studied some crane flies that his colleague Chris Steinbeck collected from the South Platte near Deckers. Shafer took several photographs of the larvae for a bench-side reference that he used while tying flies. Shafer admits that the behavior of the larvae really caught his eye. "When crane-fly larvae move around the substrate or wiggle in the water column, their segments retract into one another and their abdomen is non-symmetrical. I knew that my imitation had to be soft and squishy like the naturals. Then, all of a sudden, the design came to me and I whipped out a few prototypes. I gave them to some of my guide buddies at the Blue Quill Angler to field-test and get their input. The end result was a deadly crane-fly larva that fooled fish under a wide range of conditions. All the guides came back begging for more."

The materials Shafer uses in his Gummy Crane are a game-changer. "The combination of a two-tone abdomen (light-brown Squirmy Wormy material and brown Scud Back) in conjunction with a UV flash underbody produced the pattern that I was looking for. The biggest breakthrough was the Squirmy Worm material and the way I tied it on the hook. It's important to vary the tension on the Squirmy Worm material so the body segments appear uneven. That drives most tiers nuts (it looks poorly tied), but I cannot emphasize this enough. The irregular abdomen (as pictured) simulates the movement of a crane-fly larva. Another important addition to the Gummy Crane was wrapping the hook shank with .020 lead wire to get the fly to sink quick. I named this pattern the Gummy Crane because trout chew on it (like chewing gum) and don't want to let it go."

Shafer's Gummy Crane has saved the day many times when the bite was off or the outflows changed below Cheesman Reservoir. When there are no evident hatches and the trout are hunkered down, that's a great time to think outside the box and throw a large offering looking for an opportunistic grab. I can't even begin to tell you how many times Shafer's Gummy Crane was my "ace in the hole" when Denver Water released water from Cheesman Reservoir to meet downstream demand. There is nothing more frustrating than when the water rises, turns off-color, and is filled with debris. When things seem hopeless, try Shafer's Gummy Crane; I think you'll be pleasantly surprised with how effective it can be in dirty water.

Shafer recommends fishing his Gummy Crane as a lead fly in a tandem nymphing rig. He frequently uses tight line tactics but also fishes it underneath a strike indicator. He typically attaches his dropper fly (flies) 18 inches below the Gummy Crane and chooses them based on matching the prevailing hatches. If a midge hatch is in progress, he'll trail midge pupae; if a blue-winged olive emergence is occurring, Shafer suggests using *Baetis* nymphs or emergers; and so on. In shallow riffles the Gummy Crane doesn't require any additional weight, but in deeper runs and holes, or swifter currents, Shafer advises adding some split shot 14 to 16 inches above the Gummy Crane to get it down near the substrate.

You cannot have too many of Joe Shafer's Gummy Cranes. This is a batch that was tied by Joe Shafer himself. FORREST DORSEY

H & L Variant

(Tied by Umpqua Feather Merchants)

- **Hook:** #12–#18 Tiemco 100
- **Thread:** Black 6/0 Uni-Thread
- **Tail:** Calf-tail (body) hair
- **Abdomen:** Stripped peacock quill and peacock herl
- **Wings:** Calf-tail (body) hair
- **Hackle:** Whiting Farms brown rooster

The H & L Variant has long been a Colorado favorite when it comes to attractor dry flies. R. C. Coffman is credited with tying the first H & L Variant back in the mid-1950s. The story is told that Coffman sold so many H & L Variants to President Eisenhower that he was able to buy a house and lot (hence the name H & L) on the banks of the famed Frying Pan River near Basalt, Colorado. While that story might have been embellished a bit, the H & L Variant was truly President Eisenhower's favorite fly.

President Eisenhower thoroughly enjoyed fishing near the small community of Fraser, Colorado. The scenic Fraser Valley is bordered by Winter Park on the south and the quaint town of Tabernash on the north. President Eisenhower frequently stayed on the 3,800-acre Byers Peak Ranch adjacent to St. Louis Creek (a tributary of the Fraser River), which was owned by his buddies Aksel Nielsen and Carl Norgren. Byer's Peak Ranch was often referred to as the "Western White House" because St. Louis Creek was President Eisenhower's favorite place to fish.

The H & L Variant has a rich history in Colorado because it was President Eisenhower's favorite dry fly. The calf-hair tail and wings make it easy to see and the heavily hackled thorax area provides exceptional floatation. From large western freestones to smaller, meandering meadow streams, the H & L Variant is a good choice when trout are feeding opportunistically on surface offerings.

I first learned about the H & L Variant when I was looking through Jack Dennis's *Western Trout Fly Tying Manual* in an effort to step up my dry-fly game. Several of the patterns caught my eye—the Humpy, Royal Humpy, Royal Wulff, Adams Irresistible, Gray Wulff, and Parachute Adams (all reliable patterns for Colorado)—but for some reason the H & L Variant stood out from the crowd.

The H & L Variant is built for western waters—it floats like a cork because it is heavily hackled (oversized hackle is frequently used in true variant fashion) to ride high on the choppiest of currents. The white calf-tail wings and tail make it extremely visible under a wide range of conditions. The peacock herl adds a dash of iridescent flash that attracts nearby fish. Peacock herl has a magical fish-catching power that opportunistic trout cannot resist. Think about how effective the Prince Nymph, Halfback Nymph, Royal Wulff, Renegade, Griffith Gnat, Gray Ugly, and Pheasant Tail flies are—they all have the same common denominator: peacock herl.

Attractors like the H & L Variant are a great option in July and August, when trout have been accustomed to looking up and feeding on caddis, yellow sallies, pale morning duns, and Tricos. If you enjoy unmatching the hatch, the H & L Variant will quickly become one of your favorite flies.

After staring at a strike indicator all season long, throwing an attractor dry fly is a breath of fresh air. Attractors start to become effective toward that latter part of June, when spring runoff subsides, and remain important until the middle part of September. There is nothing more exciting than watching a trout rise from the depths of the stream and eat a large dry fly. I consider attractor fishing to be "unmatching the hatch" and typically fish them when no apparent hatches are evident. Fish that have been accustomed to looking up and feeding on the surface rarely refuse the opportunity to grab an attractor.

The most effective way to fish an H & L Variant is methodically covering the water, showing the fly to as many fish as possible. Attractors are often referred to as "searching patterns" because they allow anglers to cover a lot of different water types and speeds. Pounding the same piece of water is counterproductive with attractors, so make sure you keep probing the water systematically.

Attractors can be fished upstream, downstream, up and across or down, and across the stream. Their applications vary depending on the situation. If I am walk-wading, especially in pocket water or riffled currents, I typically fish an attractor straight upstream. But if I am fishing from an inflatable raft or drift boat pounding the stream banks, I typically fish up and across. In softer currents and glassy pools, I typically fish down and across with a reach mend so that the fly precedes the leader. Upstream casts in glassy pools can "line" fish and put them down. Adapt to each set of circumstances as you see fit.

Hell Razor Leech

(Tied by Matt McCannel)

- **Hook:** #12 Umpqua 403 BL
- **Eyes:** ⅛" black nickel, dumbbell
- **Thread:** Black UTC 70 denier
- **Tail/body:** Black pine squirrel
- **Underbody:** Black Wapsi Prism SLF Multi-Laminated Synthetic dubbing
- **Collar:** Black pine squirrel in a dubbing loop

My first eye-opening experience with leech imitations was down on the San Juan River back in the mid-1990s. I was on a busman's holiday with my good friend Matt Miles floating the stretch between the Texas Hole and the Gravel Pit. Miles and I were catching our fair share of fish on red midge larvae, Black Beauties, WD-40s, and chocolate Foam Wing Emergers, but we noticed Johnny Gomez, one of the top guides in the area, was catching a lot more fish than we were.

Every time we looked over at his boat, one of his clients had a bent rod; in some cases, they were doubled up, which was an amazing sight to see.

Miles and I were close enough to a see that Gomez was fishing with something quite large, dark in color, trailed by a smaller fly. Later that day we ran into Gomez at Abe's Fly Shop and we asked him what he catching all those fish on. Gomez said he was fishing with a rust-brown leech, tied from a pine squirrel

If you're a big fan of leech imitations, Matt McCannel's Hell Razor Leech should pique your interest. McCannel's design keeps the Hell Razor Leech riding hook point up, which is a huge advantage for the angler because it does not get hung up or snagged on submerged structure. McCannel uses a little flash to attract nearby trout but doesn't go overboard because he feels too much is often a red flag and spooks wary trout.

strip, trailing a small midge-nymph that he designed called a Desert Storm. Miles and I each picked up a few of those patterns at the fly shop and found them to be successful the following day.

Leech patterns have really become popular in Colorado in recent years. According to McCannel, head guide at Riggs Fly Shop in Ridgway, Colorado, "Leeches are an important food source for trout when they are available. Most freestone rivers and tailwaters here in Colorado have a dense population of leeches, which led me to design the Hell Razor Leech. Small leeches are one of my go-to patterns for large trout that are often wary of larger flies on the Uncompahgre River. On the Gunnison River I have had fish regurgitate leeches in the bottom of my boat, which emphasizes their importance."

McCannel designed the Hell Razor Leech to ride hook point up. This is advantageous because the fly does not get hung up on the bottom or snagged on any debris. McCannel decided to tie the Hell Razor on a jig hook, which helps ensure a good hookup in the upper jaw of the fish. "The Hell Razor Leech has a realistic profile with just the right amount of flash to entice an opportunistic grab, but not too much to spook large, wary trout. The ⅛-inch dumbbell eyes give the fly enough weight to sink fast, with limited bulk, which aids in the sink rate as well."

McCannel offers this tip on fishing leeches: "The Hell Razor Leech is a highly versatile fly that can be fished on a dead drift under an indicator, stripped as a streamer, or as a dropper under a larger dry fly. I fish the Hell Razor most of the time under an indicator, sight casting to a particular trout. I typically fish the Hell Razor as a point fly on a two-fly setup. Because the jig hook is barbless, I always tie my dropper to the eye of the Hell Razor Leech as opposed to the bend of the hook. If I am

fishing the Hell Razor Leech to a unusually large fish (over 10 pounds), I use only the leech, to avoid any mishaps with multiple flies, which ultimately can spook the fish."

Strange as it might sound, McCannel likes to fish the Hell Razor Leech underneath a hopper in a dry-and-dropper rig. His fishing style is quite unique—after casting the hopper trailed by his Hell Razor Leech, he recommends making a huge, aggressive mend. Then McCannel lets the leech sink in the water column, allows it to dead-drift for a few feet, and then he makes another huge, aggressive mend. He believes the jigging motion triggers aggressive takes.

McCannel ties the Hell Razor Leech in three different color variations: olive, black, and natural (gray). The Hell Razor leech has become one of McCannel's favorite lake flies. The versatility of this pattern makes it a good option for carp and other warmwater species.

Forrest Dorsey found success on the Williams Fork River with one of Matt McCannel's Hell Razor Leeches. During the autumn season, migratory brown trout move upstream from the Colorado River into nearby tributaries in search of areas to spawn. The pre-spawn phase typically produces some exceptional streamer fishing for anglers who enjoy the thrill and excitement of hunting for big trout.

Jungle Junkie

(Tied by Steve Maldonado)

- **Hook:** 4/0 Tiemco 600 SP
- **Eye:** Fire-red 10 mm Fish Skull Living Eyes
- **Underbody:** .030 lead wire
- **Articulation:** Fish Skull articulated shank 20 mm
- **Thread:** Semperfi 3/0 200 D
- **Body:** Chartreuse, white, and olive large northern bucktail in conjunction with fire tiger, pear, red, white magnum Flashabou, and Cobalt Sparkle Angelina Fiber
- **Vertical bands:** Black Sharpie
- **Head:** Olive, yellow, and orange Senyo's Laser Dub

No angler's fly selection is complete without a few patterns to chase toothy critters in several of Colorado's lakes and reservoirs known for their tiger muskie and northern pike fishing. In recent years tiger muskies (a non-native hybrid fish) have been stocked into several of the state's waters (Evergreen Lake, Antero, Pinewood, Big Creek Horseshoe, and Gross Reservoirs, to name only a few) to assist in the management of certain fisheries.

"Tiger muskies are considered a silent predator to help us control undesirable species that are present in some of our lakes and reservoirs," said Jeff Spohn, senior aquatic biologist for Colorado Parks and Wildlife. "These undesirable species compete with sportfish such as rainbow trout and brown trout for resources and can reduce the productivity of a body of water." White and long-nose suckers are a great example: If left uncontrolled, they can completely take over a lake or reservoir. Once the "trash fish" populations are back in check, tiger muskie are no longer stocked by Colorado Parks and Wildlife.

Colorado Parks and Wildlife's plan of attack is a brilliant way to manage the resource, with

Steve Maldonado is a pro's pro when it comes to targeting apex predators. His Jungle Junkie is a pattern that you should carry if you enjoy targeting voracious predators on the fly. Maldonado designed his Jungle Junkie to imitate a perch, which is a huge food source for tiger muskie and northern pike.

the added bonus of providing anglers with another gamefish to pursue. A tiger muskie is a northern pike and muskellunge (muskie) cross, a hybrid that is sterile and cannot reproduce. According to Colorado Parks and Wildlife, in 2019 15,000 tiger muskies were stocked in Colorado in twenty-nine different locations.

This is great news for anglers like Steve Maldonado who enjoy hunting for big predatory fish. His Jungle Junkie is another arrow in your quiver for pursuing voracious predators on the fly. "This fly came about many years before I started tying flies. I was fishing on the Bud Light Bass Championship Tour in Texas for close to 20 years. After giving it up and moving back to Colorado, where I was born and raised, I took what I learned from chasing largemouth bass and other fierce predators and adapted it to my fly-fishing tactics."

The pattern Maldonado came up with, one he ties and fishes 90 percent of the time, was something that resembled one of his favorite spinner baits. Maldonado's concoction has

Maldonado's Jungle Junkie is a good option if you enjoy pursuing pike on the fly. Northern pike of all sizes are caught in Colorado, and some upwards of 50 inches can be found in some of the state's renowned stillwater impoundments like Eleven Mile and Williams Fork Reservoirs. Pike are also targeted on the Yampa River and smaller watersheds like this one Craig Davis caught on Tarryall Creek.

proven itself time and time again for northern pike in Stagecoach, Williams Fork, Eleven Mile, Tarryall, and Spinney Reservoirs. "It's my top producer. Period. In 2021 Umpqua Feather Merchants picked up my fly and called it the Jungle Junkie because it has been equally effective for peacock bass in the Amazon." Prior to that Maldonado had been toying around with several different names, but nothing officially stuck until Umpqua named the fly. Maldonado believes that his Jungle Junkie works well for imitating a perch, which is a huge food source for northern pike and tiger muskie.

Decades ago northern pike were introduced into several of Colorado's lakes and reservoirs as a predatory fish, with the same goals in mind, but they can overtake a fishery and decimate trout populations because of their voracious appetite and ability to reproduce. The advantage to stocking tiger muskies is they are easier to control. Once their food source diminishes, they die naturally through attrition and the fishery remains balanced.

Anglers who enjoy targeting northern pike can find them in Stagecoach, Catamount, Green Mountain, Spinney, Eleven Mile, and Tarryall Reservoirs, and some escapees can be found in the streams below each stillwater impoundment. Maldonado recommends fishing the Jungle Junkie with an intermediate line on a 8- or 9-weight line. "The stainless-steel leader I use for northern pike and tiger muskie is Tyger; it's the best I've ever used. You can tie any kind of knot to it because it is as supple as any mono leader material. I've caught some really big pike and muskie and never come close to breaking it. I treat the Jungle Junkie like a jerk bait, pinching the line by the grip and giving it two or three violent jerks, then let it sink, followed by two or three hard strips, then repeat until I get a grab. When a northern pike or tiger muskie grabs it, they absolutely attack it!"

Krueger's Sculp Gulp

(Tied by Chris Krueger)

Chris Krueger was born and raised in Fort Collins, Colorado, where he grew up fishing northern Colorado's trout streams and stillwater impoundments for a variety of warmwater species. Like many of the talented tiers that are featured in these pages, Krueger starting tying flies when he was a young boy.

Krueger was blessed with a grandfather that fished with him regularly. "My grandfather opened my eyes to several different trout patterns and classics that he fished throughout his life. I spent most of the time tying classic wet and dry flies, Wulff patterns, and filling my family members' fly boxes. By the time I was in high school, I was tying commercially for local shops, cranking out quill wing extended body mayflies and hair wing dry flies."

- **Hook:** Size 4-1/0 Daiichi 2461
- **Thread:** Rusty-brown 140 denier
- **Eyes:** Yellow and black LG Lead Dumbbell
- **Tail:** Tan and brown MFC Barred Buggerbou
- **Body:** Gold UV Polar Chenille. Larger sizes use Schlappen for added profile and taper.
- **Legs:** Silicone rubber legs
- **Head:** Tan pseudo hair tapered in dubbing loop, brushed out, and wrapped behind and through eyes. Pay close attention to butt ends in the loop to be longer at the top of the loop tapering down to smaller at the bottom of the loop to maintain amounts of underfur. This will accomplish the appropriate bullethead profile and retain long fibers extending into the tail.
- *Note:* Color bars on the top of the pseudo hair for added realism or shading—Chartpack or Prismacolor markers are good options.

If you enjoy reactionary grabs or hunting for opportunistic gamefish, Chris Krueger's Sculp Gulp is a great option. It's easy to cast from a boat or perfect for the walk-wade angler that enjoys covering a lot of water. The Sculp Gulp can be fished deep on sinking line bouncing the bottom, around fallen trees, weed beds, and other submerged structure, or stripped with a faster retrieve with a floating line in the middle part of the water column.

Krueger is a well-rounded tier and angler, focusing his efforts on a wide array of gamefish including trout, bass, carp, pike, muskie, and more. "I originally designed the Sculp Gulp as a counterpart to my Darth Invader (a large, articulated offering) when a smaller, single-shank streamer was desired." Krueger ties the Sculp Gulp in a variety of colors from white to black and everything in between. He mixes things up by changing the color of the eyes, tail, body, and head. For instance, for a sculpin he uses an olive/brown tail, olive/copper body, and olive head; for a shad he uses a white/gray tail, silver body, and white/gray head; for a bluegill he uses an olive/brown tail, olive body, light-blue legs, and an olive head; and so on. He also ties a rainbow and brown trout imitation and tweaks the materials accordingly.

Krueger admits that the material selection has been a bit of an evolution over the years, and it lends itself to alterations depending on the situation and species being targeted throughout. "I felt it was important to pay close attention to the fly's profile, using materials and techniques that steelhead tiers have used for many years. I wanted to utilize material densities and butt sections of a dubbing loop to accomplish an overall large torpedo shape to the fly—mimicking the small trout and baitfish found on my local waters. By using a fur substitute on the front of the fly for consistency, I was able to control the amount of underfur with a taper in a dubbing loop, and I was able to easily alter the amount of impact water hydraulics had on other materials tied behind it. This combination allowed for the softer, more supple materials in the back to breathe life in the current, adding the illusion of movement with grizzly marabou and flash. Originally, I used prime marabou tails with small grizzly mini marabou feathers cupped on the outside to accomplish a subtle barring. Though I still do this at times when subtlety is key and a fish might have a longer, clearer look at the fly, the ease of MFC Barred Marabou is perfect when you are cranking these out because their quality of barring is second to none."

Krueger believes the impact of flash and legs and even an optional rattle are just icing on the cake to a classic baitfish shape, and materials that are resistant to teeth and torture from hooking multiple fish. The use of pseudo hair allowed the head of the fly to transition into the body for a cohesive look, rather than a clipped wool, fur, or deer-hair head. "The use of new materials over the years has found its way into this pattern, and I often find myself accomplishing different profiles and textures using foxy brushes, EP brushes, and complex loops to add new looks to this pattern. Brushes work well to keep a consistent profile on the larger sizes and Pseudo Hair is far preferred for smaller profiles due to the density of the underfur, the length of the longer fibers, and the tapered ends to the fibers you can't get in craft fur and other substitutes. They also take markers well and dry quickly when wet."

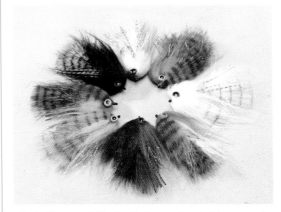

Chris Krueger's Sculp Gulp can be tied in several different colors to imitate a wide array of baitfish. Krueger tweaks his design to imitate sculpin, shad, bluegill, rainbow trout, and brown trout.

Laney's Mysis

(Tied by Joe Shafer)

- **Hook:** #14–#22 Tiemco 200 R
- **Thread:** Uni .004 clear mono
- **Abdomen:** Pearl Flashabou
- **Head:** Bright-white Antron yarn
- **Eyes:** Black medium round rubber legs
- **Hot spot:** Orange Super Hair
- **Finish:** UV epoxy or Loon Solarez

If you're a big fan of deep, bottom-release tailwaters, chances are pretty good you are familiar with mysis shrimp. Three tailraces in Colorado—the Frying Pan, Taylor, and Blue Rivers—have the reputation of growing some huge trout as a result of the Colorado Division of Wildlife (CDOW), introducing mysis shrimp into Dillon, Ruedi, and Taylor Park Reservoirs in the early 1970s. The plan of attack was to try to increase the growth rates of kokanee salmon and other resident fish in the shallow areas (bays, coves, and inlets) of the reservoirs. This strategy was based on the success that game and fish agencies had in 1949 when they introduced mysis shrimp into British Columbia's Kootenay Lake. It worked well in British Columbia, but the jury is still out in Colorado, as the results have been mixed.

In my book *Colorado Guide Flies*, I explain in great detail the unexpected challenges that the CDOW faced. Here is a recap. Early on, it was unclear whether the kokanee salmon were actually benefiting from the introduction of the mysis shrimp. It appeared that the CDOW's strategy was backfiring due to the mysis shrimp being omnivorous filter feeders,

If you frequent the Frying Pan, Blue, or Taylor Rivers, you'll want to make sure your fly boxes are loaded with Joe Shafer's Laney's Mysis. Shafer's Mysis imitation is the perfect imposter for living mysis shrimp as they exit the dam into the tailrace below.

feeding heavily on zooplankton—an important food source for juvenile trout and small kokanee salmon. As time went on, the CDOW encountered other setbacks, including the discovery that mysis shrimp are light-sensitive and thrive in water temperatures that are 57 degrees Fahrenheit or lower. This meant that as the shallow-water areas warmed, the mysis shrimp migrated to deeper water during the day to seek cooler temperatures. The mysis shrimp would return to the shallow water when the temperatures cooled down at night. As it turned out, the kokanee salmon had exactly the opposite migratory pattern, which did not allow them to benefit from the stocking of the mysis shrimp.

What the CDOW never anticipated was how much of an impact the mysis shrimp would have on the tailraces below these reservoirs. Fish that were once measured in inches were all of a sudden calculated in pounds. Mysis mania spread throughout the country and anglers flocked to the "Pan," Taylor, and Blue Rivers in search of trophy trout.

A Colorado favorite is Joe Shafer's Laney's Mysis, a proven pattern that has fooled finicky,

The Blue River is known for its mysis-fed trout. Anglers across the state come to fish the Silverthorne area in hopes of catching a trophy trout. Joe Shafer's Laney's Mysis stacks the odds in your favor of doing just that.

mysis-fed trout for nearly two decades. "I developed Laney's Mysis in the winter of 2004. My goal was to create a lifelike mysis imitation, so I began collecting shrimp from the Blue, Taylor, and Frying Pan Rivers. After carefully studying the samples, there were three things that really caught my eye. First was the pearlescent sheen along the body and tail. Strange as it might sound, the pearlescent flash was present both in and out of the water. The second important feature is the dark, prominent eyes. The third characteristic—the one I felt was most important—is the orange spot that shows through the eyes of the mysis shrimp when they are still alive."

Shafer was able to replicate these important characteristics by combining Pearl Flashabou, black, round rubber legs (medium), and orange Super Hair into his design. He finishes off the fly with a UV resin, which mimics the glass-like appearance. I asked Shafer why he calls his pattern Laney's Mysis. "I named it after my daughter Delaney. Her nickname is Laney," Shafer said.

Living mysis shrimp are transparent when they are alive in the reservoir, but they die quickly once they hit moving water in the tailrace below the dam. Close to the dam, I recommend using clear mysis shrimp patterns, but as you move downstream, you should fish white (opaque) patterns to imitate the dead shrimp. Savvy anglers choose their imitations based on the proximity of the dam, or use one clear and one opaque imitation to cover all scenarios.

According to Shafer, "There are several different ways to fish Laney's Mysis. Mysis are buoyant and good swimmers; therefore, they are found in all the parts of the water column. One of my favorite tactics is using a tandem nymph rig underneath a strike indicator, using a larger nymph as an attractor, and trailing a Laney's Mysis behind it."

Lunch Money

(Tied by Matt Bennett)

- **Hook:** #2–#4 Ahrex NS 122 Light Stinger
- **Thread:** Olive Veevus 140 denier Power Thread
- **Eyes:** Black/White Hareline Double Pupil Eyes (medium)
- **Tail/collar:** Olive Variant Hareline Black-Barred Rabbit Strips
- **Legs:** Black-Barred Olive Hareline Grizzly Flutter Legs
- **Head:** Silver Minnow Belly, white, light-olive, olive, and fluorescent Cerise Senyo's Laser Dub
- **Spots:** Black Sharpie
- **UV resin:** Loon Flow

Matt Bennett's Lunch Money fills a special niche in many anglers' fly boxes because it fools a wide variety of gamefish. Whether you're fishing on a bass pond in the Front Range; targeting toothy critters in Tarryall, Williams Fork, or Spinney Reservoirs; or chasing trout wherever they swim, the Lunch Money in a wide range of sizes and colors is as versatile as they come.

Bennett resides in Austin, Texas, but his family spends a lot of time fishing in Colorado. "We have had a family cabin in the San Juan National Forest near Durango for nearly 40 years. It's where I found my grandpa's old Berkley fiberglass fly rod, which got me interested in the sport. I've traveled up to Colorado to fish the southwestern part of the state every year since I was a teenager."

The Bennetts typically open their cabin up in late May or early June and continue using it until the snow flies in late September or early October. "When we arrive it's typically during the onset of spring runoff, the lower-elevation

If you're a die-hard streamer fanatic, you'll want to include Matt Bennett's Lunch Money in your streamer selection. It can be tied in a variety of colors to imitate several different baitfish. Favorites include rainbow trout (pictured), brown trout, black, olive, white, shad, and crawdad.

streams are running high and off-colored, and the high-country creeks near our cabin are still snowed in. Sometimes we get lucky and can float the upper San Juan River near Pagosa Springs during the early stages of runoff. As a general rule, we go fish the Dolores River below McPhee Reservoir, a challenging tailwater that requires a lot of skill to master. The Lunch Money has truly accounted for some great fish in southwest Colorado, typically at dawn or dusk or on rainy, overcast days when the fish aren't quite as skittish."

Bennett is a full-time professional fly tier. His company, Fly Geek Custom Flies, specializes in tying flies for predatory fish. According to Bennett, "The Lunch Money was created out of the need for a 2-to-3-inch bite-sized baitfish streamer for the Texas Hill Country." Bennett is quick to give credit to Charlie Craven for inspiring his design. "I based the original fly off Charlie Craven's Gonga streamer, with a few changes."

Like most great patterns, they evolve over time and go through a series of modifications to improve their design. "The Lunch Money was originally tied hook-down with larger legs, spun craft fur head, and just a tail (no wrapping for a profile transition) on a TMC 8089 #12. After coming across Laser Dub a few years back, I incorporated that amazing material into the flies' design to give it a nice, translucent profile in the water with just the right amount of sheen. I also flipped the fly to ride hook-up at that time, so I could use a slower retrieve without hanging up on the bottom. Originally, I trimmed the head to shape but later started brushing the Laser Dub back instead, ending up with a similar shape with more water-pushing capabilities. I currently tie the Lunch Money on a Ahrex NS122 (sizes 2–6), which is a great hook."

It won't take you long to figure out why the Lunch Money is so effective. The rabbit Zonker strip and Sili Legs bring the pattern to life, and the Laser Dub produces the perfect shape and translucency of a baitfish in the water. The black-and-white eyeballs put the finishing touch on this magnificent pattern. I cannot even begin to tell you how many fish I have caught on this fly over the past few years.

Bennett ties the Lunch Money in several color variations including rainbow trout, brown trout, shad, olive, white, tan/white, crawdad, and black. "The original tan/white color is still my go-to just about anywhere, but I'm also a big fan of the rainbow trout color. In southwestern Colorado, where I tend to fish the most, I fish a Lunch Money on a 9-foot 6-weight rod. During spring runoff, I'll fish a Lunch Money on a short leader (3–4 feet) with a sink-tip line. Later in the year, when the river gets low and clear, I'll lengthen the leader and use a floating line. Sometimes I opt to fish with two Lunch Moneys, using a lighter-colored version as my lead fly, trailed by a darker variation, until I find what the fish are responding to. Short, quick strips are usually the name of the game, but I recommend changing your retrieve from time to time to let the fish tell you what they want!"

Matt Bennett's Lunch Money is a proven producer throughout the state of Colorado. This large rainbow was fooled with an olive Lunch Money near an undercut bank.

Manhattan Midge

(Tied by Forrest Dorsey)

- **Hook:** #18–#24 Tiemco 2488
- **Bead:** Silver-lined glass bead (extra small)
- **Thread:** Black 12/0 Veevus
- **Abdomen:** Black 12/0 Veevus
- **Rib:** UTC copper wire (small for 18–20, extra small for 22)
- **Wing:** Prism White Glamour Madiera
- **Thorax:** Peacock herl

Forrest Dorsey was born in Littleton, Colorado, and caught his first fish on a fly rod when he was 7 years old. Growing up he spent endless hours fishing the South Platte River (Deckers and Cheesman Canyon) pursuing some of the toughest trout in the country. "Early on, I knew I was destined to become a tailwater junkie. I started tying flies when I was 8 years old, learning how to tie South Platte favorites like the Brassie, Miracle Nymph, WD-40, RS 2, Mercury Midge, Black Beauty, Top Secret Midge, Mercury Flashback Pheasant Tail, and so many more. I was fortunate to have my father take me under his wing and teach me the secrets of the trade at an early age," Dorsey said.

Success on any western tailwater begins by having a thorough selection of midges. One of the most popular midges in Colorado the past few years has been the Manhattan Midge. "The Manhattan Midge was one of the first patterns I designed to fool selective Rocky Mountain trout. The Manhattan Midge was developed in New York City in a tiny apartment where

The Manhattan Midge is quickly becoming one of Colorado's favorite small fly offerings. The Manhattan Midge works best during the height of a midge hatch, when super-selective trout are focusing their attention on pupae. Dorsey's design incorporates a segmented abdomen in conjunction with some flashy materials (Prism White Glamour Madeira, peacock herl, and a silver-lined glass bead) that breathe life and help separate it from the crowd.

I was living while my wife was attending law school. Moving from Colorado to New York City was a dramatic change, so I often found myself tying flies to stay connected to the sport."

After arriving to the Big Apple, Dorsey quickly landed a job with Orvis Company in New York City to pursue a livelihood in the fishing industry and soon thereafter launched his online business—Tailwater Junkie—to supply flies to other passionate anglers who enjoy fooling tough trout on tiny flies. "The Manhattan Midge is a souped-up hybrid of my father's Top Secret Midge, Mercury Black Beauty, and Mercury Blood Midge that incorporates the best attributes of each pattern. It has a slim profile, segmented body, a flashy wing, peacock collar that breathes life, and a clear silver-lined bead to mimic the trapped air in the thorax during emergence. The Manhattan Midge has become a guide favorite on the South Platte River, including Cheesman, Deckers, Eleven Mile Canyon, and the Charlie Meyers State Wildlife Area, and is beginning to spread to eastern tailwaters."

The Manhattan Midge is equally effective on the state's freestone streams as well. Industry professionals like Jason Booth of Gunnison River Guides rely heavily on the Manhattan Midge to fool the midge feeders on the Gunnison River. "I have been a fly-fishing guide on the Gunnison River for over 25 years. The Manhattan Midge is one of our top-producing patterns when midges are emerging. It is the perfect attractor," says Booth.

Dorsey encourages everyone to tie his Manhattan Midge in red, brown, olive, and purple. He also ties a flashback variation that incorporates a strip of Mylar tinsel on the topside of the abdomen to enhance the gas-bubble effect and translucency of an emerging midge. Dorsey offers this bit of advice with regard to tying a realistic abdomen and keeping the thorax thin and sparse. "It's important to segment the body with several even wraps of copper wire and to keep the peacock-herl collar small. Using peacock eyes (instead of strung peacock herl) allows you to select the piece you want for whatever size you are tying. The smaller sizes are on the base of the feather, and as you progress up the stem, they become larger and fluffier, which works well for bigger sizes."

Midge feeders take the Manhattan Midge with confidence. "The Manhattan Midge fishes well year-round, but it is especially productive during the height of a midge hatch when you see suspended trout sweeping back and forth eating pupae. I recommend tying it in a variety of sizes to imitate the various midge hatches you'll encounter throughout the season. For instance, I use a size 18 when the big spring midge is hatching and use a size 20 to 22 when smaller midges are emerging later in the year. Strange as it might sound, a black Manhattan Midge works well as a drowned Trico or black ant in many watersheds."

This thick-bodied Yampa River rainbow couldn't resist a size 20 black Manhattan Midge during the onset of a morning midge hatch. When you see midge adults flying in the air or streamside, it's safe to assume the trout are feeding on midge pupae. When a midge hatch is in progress, savvy anglers snip off their larvae imitations and swap them out for pupae.

Matt's Midge

(Tied by Matt Miles)

- **Hook:** #18–#26 Tiemco 101
- **Thread:** Black 8/0 Uni-Thread
- **Abdomen:** Black 8/0 Uni-Thread
- **Wing:** White Z-Lon
- **Hackle:** Whiting Farms grizzly rooster

Matt Miles moved to Granby, Colorado, from Lynchburg, Virginia, when he was 18 years old to pursue a lifelong dream of becoming a professional fly-fishing guide. I met Miles on the Williams Fork River in 1994 after noticing that he was fishing there several days a week. One morning I struck up a casual conversation with Miles and asked him if he was on vacation. He was quick to reply, "No . . . I just moved to Colorado . . . my goal is to become a fly-fishing guide." I suggested

that we should fish together one evening after my guide trip and get to know each other.

The following week we fished at the Sun Set Ranch, a stretch of water on the Colorado River downstream from the small community of Parshall. Immediately I knew there was something special about this young man. He had incredible people skills and his angling abilities were impressive to say the least.

At the time, I co-owned an outfitter with Mark LoCurto called Master Angler, based

Matt's Midge imitates a single, newly hatched adult. Its pronounced wing makes it visible on the water, which is a huge advantage for tailwater enthusiasts who enjoy fishing with tiny dry flies. Miles recommends carrying Matt's Midge in sizes 18 to 24 to be prepared for a variety of situations. A size 18 works well in the spring when the larger midges (big spring midge) are emerging, and sizes 20 to 24 are good options during the remainder of the year.

out of Parker, Colorado. I asked Miles if he would consider working for us, and he gladly accepted the position. When I became a partner in the Blue Quill Angler in 2001, Miles moved to the Front Range and joined the team of professionals in Evergreen, Colorado, where he helped us guide customers on the South Platte, Arkansas, Blue, Colorado, and Williams Fork Rivers.

It didn't take me long to figure out Miles was a gifted fly tier as well. The fruits of his labor were for his guided trips and personal fishing excursions on a wide array of western trout streams. "The idea of tying Matt's Midge came to me in the late 1990s after a trip to the San Juan River in northern New Mexico. At that time there were only a handful of reliable adult midge patterns available, not to mention you needed the eyesight of an osprey to see them on the water. After the frustration of trying to locate my fly during the height of a midge hatch, the idea for Matt's Midge came to me. Adult midges have prominent wings, but none of the patterns I was using had incorporated wings into their design. So I tied an imitation with a white Z-Lon wing to look like a newly hatched adult on the water. The Z-Lon

Matt Miles fooled this brown trout on the Williams Fork River with a Matt's Midge. Selective surface feeders eat Matt's Midge with confidence because its silhouette closely resembles a newly hatched adult trying to dry its wings before it flies off the water.

wing was extremely helpful when it came to locating the fly."

Matt's Midge has since become a Colorado favorite when it comes to enticing surface feeders that are keying on adult midges. Miles is one of the best dry-fly anglers that I have ever had the pleasure to fish with. He is always willing to offer some solid advice to improve your game. "The biggest thing I see anglers doing wrong is they cast their flies too far upstream from the rising fish they want to catch. Casting 5 or 10 feet above your target, then having to mend, usually pulls the fly out of the fishes' feeding lane. I recommend placing the fly 18 inches to 2 feet upstream from the rising fish so you don't have to make any adjustments on the water. Once the fly drifts past the fish, immediately pick it up and recast. Whenever possible, I recommend presenting the fly down and across with a reach mend to a rising fish. Trout that see a lot of flies and fishing pressure are often leader-shy. That's why I show them the fly first and not the leader."

Miles says he dead-drifts Matt's Midge most of the time, but sometimes he'll think outside the box and skitter it. "One trick I learned when fishing in a dense midge hatch in the evening, especially when the light is low and the glare is high, is putting on a size 18 Hi-Vis Matt's Midge (has a bright-orange wing), then trailing a smaller white-wing version behind it with 12 inches of tippet. The fish will frequently eat the bigger variety for a midge cluster, but more important, it helps you locate the smaller midge."

Miles moved back to Lynchburg, Virginia, in 2003 to start a family and open his own outfitting company called Matt Miles Fly Fishing. He has his captain's license and specializes in fooling a variety of gamefish, including trout, bass, stripers, and muskie. Miles returns to Colorado frequently to fish all the streams he once guided on.

Mayer's Mini Leech

(Tied by Landon Mayer)

- **Hook:** #14–#16 Tiemco 2488H
- **Thread:** Olive UTC 70 denier
- **Wing:** Olive micro pine squirrel strip
- **Body:** Olive Krystal Flash
- **Collar:** Olive ostrich herl

Landon Mayer's Mini Leech is one of the most popular patterns to hit the fly-fishing industry in recent years. In different sizes and colors, Mayer's Mini Leech is as versatile as they come because it fools a wide range of gamefish from trout to carp and everything in between. The beauty of Mayer's Mini Leech is that it can be fished a number of different ways, tailoring your tactics to a specific location. For instance, on rivers and streams you may opt to dead-drift, strip, or swing a Mayer's Mini Leech into the desired structure. Still-water enthusiasts, on the other hand, might choose to suspend Mayer's Mini Leech off a strike indicator or strip it with a variety of retrieves. The best advice I can give you is not to get trapped in a rut with a "one size fits all" mentality, but instead be willing to experiment with your tactics and techniques based on the prevailing conditions.

Mayer is a big fan of using his Mini Leech during the high-water season. "Leeches are an important part of a trout's diet, especially in high-water conditions. Similar to aquatic worms, leeches are often swept off the river's edge and stream bottom, supplying nearby

Mayer's Mini Leech has created a lot of buzz in the fishing industry as of late. Its design is simple but effective, making it one of the most popular leech imitations in recent memory. Mayer's Mini Leech can be dead-drifted underneath a strike indicator or swung in the current. Another option is to fish it like a conventional streamer with a slow retrieve.

fish with an easy, non-escaping food supply. While some leeches are large in size, exceeding 1 inch, there are just as many that are less than an inch long. I designed the Mini Leech to match the small freshwater leeches that trout feed on in tailwaters, freestones, and still waters."

Mayer's design is simple but effective—but don't let that fool you! "The micro pine squirrel strip is attached in one location, near the eye of the hook, which allows it to undulate in the current. Combine this with a fluffy ostrich herl collar and you really have something that breathes life. The Krystal Flash seals the deal with some added sparkle as it wiggles in the current."

Mayer is a seasoned veteran when it comes to fishing South Park's stillwater impoundments. You'll find Mayer fishing Antero and Spinney Reservoirs several days a week during the late-spring and summer months. Wind can be a curse in South Park, but savvy anglers know that a little chop is never a bad thing. "For the stillwater bite, it really doesn't matter what season it is—most important, you should fish when there is a little wind. There's a fine line between a stiff breeze and a heavy wind in South Park, however. But with a little wind, you have pulsating or undulating movement that can be a huge advantage when you're using a Mini Leech. Rigging can be done a multitude of ways. You can attach a Mini Leech as a lead fly with an anchor fly below it, or one or two Mini Leeches can be fished underneath a strike indicator with a split shot above the flies. Sometimes I'll forgo the split shot and use one Bead Head Mini Leech (weighted) in conjunction with an unweighted version to enhance the jigging action of the trailing fly."

Another tactic is to trail a Mini Leech off a large streamer. It's a good idea to fish with one weighted and one unweighted fly and mix up the colors. For instance, you might use a weighted white streamer as the lead fly and trail a darker Mini Leech behind it. I find more times than not, a trout that ambushes a tandem streamer rig opts to eat the small, trailing fly. Mayer couldn't agree more. "Another one of my favorite ways to utilize the Mini Leech is trailing it off a large streamer. More times than not, a big trout decides to chase your large streamer to the bank but it simply won't commit. That's why trailing a smaller Mini Leech behind it works well. The reason you can get away with this strategy is that the many leeches are unweighted, which maximizes their movement and frequently entices a strike."

If you enjoy targeting a carp on a fly, a Mini Leech is a great option. "When hunting carp on the fly, I like using Mini Leeches. Not only does it imitate a natural leech, it can also represent crayfish, swimming nymphs, baitfish, and more. In deep waters I prefer my rust-colored Mini Leech Jig Radiant to imitate falling or injured crayfish or bottom-clinging leeches. In shallow-water bays or the edges of the river, I will double up. To increase my success, I use a dark (black/rust) Mini Leech Jig and allow it to fall to the substrate, creating a puff in the sand to trigger a carp."

Landon Mayer is one of the top stillwater authorities in Colorado. His Mini Leech is a pattern that he relies heavily upon when he is hunting for giant trout. MICHELLE MAYER

Mayhem Jig Nymph (Natural Variant)

(Tied by Brian Kelso)

- **Hook:** #10–#20 Hanak H 400 BL
- **Bead:** 2.5–4.0 mm silver slotted tungsten, matched to hook size
- **Thread:** Blue-dun 70 denier
- **Tail:** Medium Speckled Pardo Coq de Leon and #2 Fl. Pink Datum Glo Brite Floss
- **Body:** Natural Stripped Polish Quill and Loon UV Clear Fly Finish (Thin)
- **Thorax:** Dark-brown Angora goat, tied in dubbing loop. Fibers cut to approximately ¼" in length.

Brian Kelso is one of Colorado's top authorities when it comes to Euro nymphing. Kelso is a Colorado native and began fly fishing when he was 12 years old. He is a graduate of Western State College (Gunnison), where he got a great education but also reaped the benefits of getting a PhD in fly fishing from some of the pickiest trout in the West. Most anglers would agree—if you can consistently catch trout on the Taylor River and some of the area's fickle freestone streams, you'll succeed just about anywhere in Colorado.

Kelso started his fly-fishing career at the Blue Quill Angler in 2010. He fished in his first fly-fishing competition at the 2012 America's Cup in Vail, Colorado, and has been passionate about competitive fly fishing and European nymphing techniques ever since. Kelso teaches European nymphing classes at the Blue Quill Angler, which has provided another outlet for him to share his passion for the sport.

Kelso is also an avid fly tier and fly designer. One of Kelso's most popular patterns is the Mayhem Jig Nymph. "The Mayhem Jig was originally tied in the summer of 2012 but did not come into fruition until the 2013 Fly Fishing Team USA National Championships in Basalt, Colorado. The Mayhem Jig Nymph

Jig nymphs like Brian Kelso's pattern have become popular in recent years. His Mayhem Jig Nymph can be nymphed underneath a strike indicator or used with traditional Euro nymphing tactics.

performed quite well on most of the river sessions (Roaring Fork and Frying Pan Rivers) but most notably for the Frying Pan River. On this session thirty-seven fish were landed, many to hand on the Mayhem Jig Nymph. Since then, countless fish have fallen to the pattern throughout the South Platte drainage and the state of Colorado. The Mayhem Jig is now produced by Umpqua Feather Merchants and can be found in several specialty fly shops throughout Colorado.

According to Kelso, "The Mayhem Jig Nymph incorporates the simplicity of a typical Euro-style fly pattern while still being an imitative pattern. As the name implies, it works great for mayfly nymphs. Depending on the size and color, it works great for blue-winged olives, PMDs, and green drakes. The natural variation works great as a general attractor year-round, but particularly through the colder late winter/spring months."

Kelso developed two pattern variations of the Mayhem Jig Nymph that he strongly recommends. He tweaks the color of the bead (copper), thread (rusty brown), tail (#8, Fl. Sunburst Datum Glo Brite Floss), and body

Kelso's Mayhem Jig Nymph is a proven favorite on the South Platte River near Deckers. It is especially effective in swifter currents and pocket water, where opportunistic brown trout are eager to eat bigger offerings.

(Ginger Stripped Polish Quill) to create a ginger version. For an olive version, incorporate a copper bead, olive-brown thread #4, Fluorescent Flame Datum Glo Brite Floss, and an olive Stripped Polish Quill into the design.

Kelso believes that the material makeup of his pattern is what makes it so effective. "Coq de Leon is a staple tailing fiber in the Euro world—and with good reason. It is quite durable but a thin enough material for sparse mayfly tails. Euro flies also often incorporate hot spots. This is almost always a fluorescent and/or a UV material. The Datum Glo Brite is a great option for incorporating hot spots and comes in a variety of bright, vibrant, and fluorescent colors. Traditionally hot spots are tied in at the collar of the fly, but the Mayhem incorporates the hot spot within the tail of the fly for a slightly less obtrusive look. Polish quills provide amazing segmentation for fly tiers and give the fly a realistic look. Polish quills can be delicate, so coating them with Loon UV resin provides increased durability. For the thorax, Angora goat gives a nice buggy look, while still giving the fly a relatively natural appearance."

Kelso admits there are several ways to fish the Mayhem Jig Nymph. "The Mayhem Jig can be fished a variety of ways, and the water type will dictate which approach you should take. In faster, shallow, riffle water, a heavier-sized Mayhem will prove best on the tag position with a lighter offering off the point. This technique/setup is also great for pocket water— but don't be afraid to throw a single fly in tight pocket water situations. For deeper runs or plunge pools, particularly if suspended fish are present, switching your anchor fly to your point can be deadly. This will give you more of a vertical presentation where one fly (anchor) is near or on the bottom and the other (tag) drifts farther up into the water column where suspended fish key in on emergers."

Meat Whistle

(Tied by John Barr)

- **Hook:** #3/0–#1/0 Gamakatsu 90-degree jig hook
- **Cone:** Silver 3/0 large, 2/0 medium, 1/0 small
- **Thread:** 140-denier Ultra Thread
- **Body:** Diamond Braid
- **Wing:** Rabbit strip
- **Legs:** Sili Legs
- **Flash:** Flashabou
- **Collar:** Marabou

John Barr is one of the top fly designers in the world. Barr's innovation is driven by his love and passion for the outdoors. In his book *Barr Flies*, he states, "Bass fishing has been a passion of mine for over 30 years and I spend about 75 days a year fishing for them, mostly in my ponds, which contain both largemouth and smallmouths. I fish both conventional and fly tackle for bass, often alternating between the two. I'll kick along in my float tube with a casting rod on one side and a fly rod on the other, and whatever my mood or the situation dictates, use one or the other."

Barr admits he enjoys the sound of a level-wind casting reel and the ultimate challenge of placing a jig into structure, overhanging brush, and other obstacles that bass call their home. Barr makes it clear though—he is a fly fisherman at heart. Barr began developing the Meat Whistle back in 2002 in an effort to create something similar to jig and trailer that many conventional bass anglers use. After several years of experimentation, Barr felt like he had perfected the bass pattern he was looking for.

"For two spring seasons I fished the Meat Whistle and jig and trailer head-to-head by

You can never have too many of Barr's Meat Whistles in your streamer selection. Whether you're chasing pike, wipers, carp, bass, or trout, the Meat Whistle is one of those patterns you can rely on day in and day out.

switching off between the two after every fish. I was thrilled. The Meat Whistle caught the same size and amount of fish as the jig and trailer. In fact, at times the fly caught more big fish than the jig and trailer. I was ecstatic that I had designed a fly that could fish head-to-head with one of the most lethal bass lures ever." Barr named his pattern the Meat Whistle because it seemed to attract (call in) a lot of big fish.

Barr's design is simple but effective. He uses a Gamakatsu jig hook with a cone head to get the fly to sink quickly. Barr avoided using lead eyes because he felt they collected aquatic foliage and believed the cone produced a better-looking pattern. Barr incorporated rabbit and marabou into the design to breathe life, and Sili Legs and Flashabou to enhance the fly's movement and flash.

In a variety of sizes and colors, Barr's Meat Whistle consistently fools several different species of gamefish in Colorado (and all over the world). Black, olive, white, and rust Meat Whistles are deadly trout producers. Smallmouth and largemouth bass cannot resist black, olive, and rust variations. To date, the biggest largemouth bass I have ever caught was on an olive Meat Whistle. Carp often fall victims to crawdad Meat Whistles because they love to eat crayfish. Pike absolutely hammer white Meat Whistles with a vengeance, which rounds things off nicely.

Barr typically fishes Meat Whistles with a 5- or 6-weight line depending on the wind. He recommends using a floating line instead of a sink tip or sinking line. Barr starts with a 9-foot 0X tapered nylon leader, then cuts off 2 feet of the regular monofilament and attaches a couple feet of 0X fluorocarbon. The retrieve varies depending on the gamefish you are targeting. A fast retrieve works well on pike, but for carp, a slower presentation that mimics a crayfish hopping along the bottom is deadly. A middle-of-the-road philosophy is perfect for trout, but don't be afraid to experiment with your tactics and techniques until you find something that works.

I frequently fish with tandem streamer rigs, using a white Meat Whistle as my lead fly (attractor) and trail a smaller offering behind it, typically a darker-colored pattern like an olive or gray Barr's Slumpbuster. I'll cast the two-fly tandem rig tight to structure and begin stripping the flies, watching the white Meat Whistle (locator fly) looking for any evidence that a fish is getting ready to grab my fly. The take can occur when the fly is moving or when the fly is sinking in between strips, which is often overlooked by many anglers.

Barr offers this advice: "A significant percentage of the takes occur when the fly is sinking with no retrieve. Watch the end of your fly line, as if you were nymph fishing, for signals of a take. If the line tip moves, it is probably a fish eating your fly. Bass will hold on to this fly for a while before rejecting it, so it must feel fairly lifelike to them." That's why a locator fly is so important: It gives you the upper hand and allows you to watch your flies. If you see a flash or movement near your fly, assume the fish has eaten it, and set the hook.

Barr's Meat Whistle is a pattern that so many die-hard streamer aficionados have come to rely on over the years. Barr recommends filling your streamer boxes with several different colors including black (pictured), chartreuse, olive, virile crayfish, and white because they each play a significant role based on the prevailing conditions and the gamefish you intend to target.

Mimic Hopper

(Tied by Chris Johnson)

- **Hook:** #8–#12 Tiemco 5212
- **Thread:** Brown Veevus 10/0
- **Body:** Pale-yellow deer body hair
- **Rib:** Brown Veevus 10/0
- **Wing:** Brown Whiting Farms hen saddle
- **Overwing:** Yellow and tan spun CDC
- **Head and collar:** Natural deer body hair
- **Legs:** Yellow and camel Uni-Flexx
- **Thorax:** Tan or natural spun CDC

I grew up fishing with Joe's Hopper and Dave's Hopper because they were two of the most reliable imitations of their time. As a young man, I can honestly say I used more of Joe's Hopper because they were much easier to tie. Dave's Hopper can frustrate the best of tiers because producing a well-tied spun deer-hair head and collar is no easy task. I learned how to tie Joe's Hopper from Jack Dennis's *Western Trout Fly Tying Manual* (Volume 1). I tied oodles of them for my fly boxes in a variety of sizes. I still reminisce about fooling a beautiful rainbow trout on the Blue River

with one of the first hoppers I tied . . . it still brings a grin to my face nearly 50 years later.

Modern-day innovation has led us to some incredible hopper patterns in recent years. Natural furs and feathers, in conjunction with a few synthetic materials, produce realistic flies that float better, breathe life, and remain durable even when they get punished by aggressive trout. Some of my favorite hopper imitations include Craven's Charlie Boy Hopper, Stalcup's Hopper, and Johnson's Mimic Hopper. Chris Johnson's Mimic Hopper is arguably one of the most popular hopper patterns in recent years.

Chris Johnson's Mimic Hopper is one of the most realistic hoppers I've seen. Johnson is known for his use of natural materials when he designs flies. The deer-hair head and abdomen, in conjunction with a beautiful wing, provide the proper silhouette of a hopper, and the CDC helps the fly breathe life and assists in high floatation. The Uni-Flexx legs add motion that closes the deal on discerning trout.

Chris Johnson resides in Round Rock, Texas, but comes to Colorado often. Johnson spends a lot of time in southern Colorado and is also a registered outfitter in the Centennial State. "The southern rivers of the Centennial State are largely unsung when compared to the renowned trout fisheries of the Front Range. However, rivers such as the Rio Grande and the Conejos are worthy of every fly angler's attention. Historically, Rio Grande cutthroat were the only trout that swam in the waters of the Rio Grande drainage. Unfortunately, they now primarily persist in high-elevation lakes and streams. It was my pursuit of this little native trout that inspired the creation of the Mimic Hopper. What began as a single exploration in the backcountry became a lifelong pursuit. Throughout my entire life, my family has owned land in Colorado. Though Texas will forever be my home, the ties to Colorado are strong. Some of my fondest childhood memories were made in the Rio Grande basin. Now I am creating new ones with my own children in some of the same streams. I consider myself blessed to have beheld rare fish in rare places, and I pray that future generations are granted the same opportunity."

Chris Johnson enticed this stunning Rio Grande cutthroat to eat one of his Mimic Hoppers on a small stream in southern Colorado. The Mimic Hopper can be dead-drifted or twitched to impart the action of its lifelike counterpart. CHRIS JOHNSON

Johnson shared with me that the Mimic Hopper was designed out of his personal desire to present a hopper pattern that was equally elegant and effective. With the exception of the legs, the entire fly is constructed from natural materials. "This gives the Mimic Hopper an incredibly lifelike appearance—one that few fish can refuse. As is the case with most of the dry flies I design, the Mimic Hopper has an ample amount of CDC used in the thorax and underwing. This causes the fly to float like a cork and enhances the silhouette of the fly from the fishes' point of view. The added motion of CDC helps the fly to overcome the scrutiny of discerning trout, which ultimately means more fish to the net! The deer-hair body and head on the fly add a classic look while providing excellent flotation. As for the legs, the Uni-Flexx material resists breakage and offers the closest color match to the genuine article. Lastly, if you want to create the ultimate hopper profile, it must have a wing. The mottled hen saddle feather adds the finishing touch of realism to the effective pattern," Johnson explains.

In addition to being one of the country's most innovative fly tiers, Johnson is a great guide and instructor. "The Mimic Hopper can be twitched, popped, or dead-drifted depending on the intended target species. The Mimic Hopper has caught more than its fair share of trout, but it is equally at home in warmwater destinations. Bass and panfish simply cannot ignore this fly, and the strikes are often violent. The fly also makes a fantastic dry attractor when a hopper-dropper situation is the desired rig. No matter the challenge, this fly is up to the task. From bow-and-arrow casts to rising cutthroat in Colorado to pounding creek banks for panfish in Texas, the Mimic Hopper adds a touch of class to your hopper box and will likely earn a permanent place in your arsenal!"

Mini-Merger

(Tied by Dick Shinton)

- **Hook:** #16–#24 Tiemco 2488
- **Thread:** Brown-olive 70 denier UTC
- **Tail/shuck:** Amber Z-Lon
- **Abdomen:** Stripped natural peacock herl
- **Thorax:** Olive-brown Ice Dub
- **Wing case/Legs:** Light-brown Antron overlaid with Opal Mirage tinsel

Mayflies have been the heart and soul of fly-fishing adventures for generations. The three stages of a mayfly's development—nymph, dun, and spinner—fuel more fly-fishing fantasies than any other aquatic insect known to mankind. The transformation from nymph to dun is frequently referred to as an emerger, but it is not labeled as part of a mayfly's life cycle. Emergence occurs when the thorax (wing case) splits open and the adult (dun) pulls itself from the nymphal shuck.

Trout feed heavily on emergers because they are extremely vulnerable and provide an easy meal with minimal effort. My streamside observation leads me to believe that trout feeding on mayfly emergers can eat a half dozen or more per minute during the peak of a hatch. This might seem like a bit of an exaggeration, but trust me: I have witnessed this several times with my own two eyes.

Dick Shinton's Mini-Merger stacks the odds in your favor when blue-winged olives or pale morning duns are hatching and the trout feed selectively on emergers. Shinton is a senior guide for Laughing Grizzly Fly Shop in Longmont, Colorado, which is less than 40 minutes

Dick Shinton's Mini-Merger is a nice addition to any angler's fly box. The Mini-Merger is a great option during the height of a blue-winged olive or pale morning dun emergence when trout are keyed on mayfly emergers. The Mini-Merger can be fished in a tandem nymphing rig or used as a dropper off a dry fly.

from the entrance of Rocky Mountain National Park. "As a guide on the small streams in Rocky Mountain National Park, I rely on the Mini-Merger from ice-off to freeze-up to catch selective trout that are feeding on mayflies. The Mini-Merger is one of my go-to patterns on tailwaters as well. I regularly fish the Frying Pan, Big Thompson, South Platte in Eleven Mile Canyon, Taylor, and other tailwaters for my own enjoyment. I designed Mini-Merger to imitate the small mayfly emergers on all of those watersheds. I'll be the first to admit that the Mini-Merger is strongly influenced by Charlie Craven's fly patterns and techniques. While there are many fly patterns available to meet any fishing situation, I prefer catching trout on my own patterns, especially simple-to-tie guide flies like this one," says Shinton.

Shinton is a big fan of adding a little flash to his patterns (reflective or UV materials) to help catch the fish's eye. Like all good tiers, every one of Shinton's patterns goes through rigorous field testing and a series of modifications to improve the fly before he's happy with the final product.

"I selected the materials for the Mini-Merger for several reasons. Amber Z-Lon is a good match for the trailing shuck of most mayflies. The shuck is usually partially collapsed and thinner than most anglers realize. It's my opinion that most emerger patterns have too much bulk in the shuck; that's why I use only eight to twelve fibers depending on the hook size. I rarely tie this fly larger than a size 20 for blue-winged olives, but do upsize it a bit for pale morning duns. Stripped peacock herl provides a realistic segmented body that closely resembles the naturals. I recommend using dyed peacock herl (yellow) for the pale morning duns to lighten up the abdomen a bit. The olive-brown Ice Dub in the thorax adds properties that attract nearby fish, and the narrow strip of Opal Mirage tinsel over the wing case

reflects light, simulating trapped gases in the thorax prior to emergence."

During the initial stages of a hatch, the Mini-Merger can be fished in a tandem nymphing rig behind an attractor nymph. Shinton likes to trail the Mini-Merger off a size 16-to-18 Pheasant Tail Nymph or something similar, as he believes the larger nymphs draw attention to his emerger. Shinton really enjoys fishing his Mini-Merger trailed off a dry fly. "During active hatches I fish the Mini-Merger as a dropper behind a dun imitation. A size 20 or 22 works well with a comparable-size adult without pulling the point fly under the water. The Mini-Merger naturally sinks a few inches under the surface where the real bugs are swimming to the top. In the beginning stage of a hatch, when porpoising trout are taking emergers, they eat this fly with abandon. As their heads start poking up taking duns, the fish still take the emerger a large percentage of the time. Nothing earth-shattering here, but this fly does work remarkably well when mayflies are hatching."

Kim Dorsey enticed this outstanding brown trout to eat one of Dick Shinton's Mini-Mergers during an afternoon blue-winged olive hatch on the South Platte River. The "olives" that hatch in the fall are one to two sizes smaller than those that hatch in the spring, so anglers should adjust their fly size accordingly.

Para Iwan-e-Dun

(Tied by Phil Iwane)

- **Hook:** #16–#22 Tiemco 2488
- **Thread:** Light-olive 16/0 Veevus
- **Tail:** Dun tailing fibers
- **Abdomen:** 10–15-pound mono, wrapped with tying thread, then coated with UV resin
- **Wing:** Light Dun McFlylon
- **Thorax:** BWO Superfine
- **Hackle:** Whiting Farms medium dun rooster

Spring and fall typically produce some of the best dry-fly fishing of the year in Colorado. By the latter part of March, scores of rising trout feast on blue-winged olives each afternoon between 1 and 3 p.m. on both the state's noted tailwaters and freestones. The "olive" hatches continue to remain strong until the onset of spring runoff, which typically occurs during the middle part of May. Autumn hatches begin in mid-September and last until the latter part of November. During the fall, precipitation-fed freestone streams are the lowest of the year, providing anglers with consistent dry-fly opportunities. Deep-bottom release tailwaters provide similar conditions as the need for downstream agricultural demand becomes less important in the fall.

Blue-winged olives (duns) are characterized by their opaque, upright wing; two or three tails (depending on the species); a sleek, curved olive body; six delicate legs; and a small pair of hind wings (missing in some species). Fly tiers have developed several unique patterns to imitate the dun—Catskill-type dry flies, thorax duns, no hackles, Comparaduns, and parachute varieties—all of which have

Phil Iwane's attention to detail is what makes his patterns so unique. From the realistic tail and curved olive abdomen to the well-proportioned wing and parachute-style hackle, this mayfly dun imitation is about as good as it gets. The Parachute Iwan-e-Dun consistently fools the most discerning trout you'll encounter during the height of a blue-winged olive hatch.

fooled selective trout all over the United States. Each variation has its advantages and disadvantages with regard to visibility, durability, and the way the fly sits in the surface film.

Most fly tiers agree that the single-most important element in tying a mayfly dun is creating a realistic silhouette of the wing. Parachute patterns allow the body to sit lower in the surface film, providing a more realistic impression to the fish. The upright wing produces the important silhouette that dun imitations require, but furthermore, the wing makes the fly much easier to see and follow on the water.

One of the new trending blue-winged olive patterns is Phil Iwane's Para Iwan-e-Dun. "When I designed the Para Iwan-e-Dun several years ago, the idea was to develop a mayfly dun imitation that looks realistic, has an extended body, floats well, and has a large hook gape that assists in better hookups, in comparison to conventional blue-winged olive patterns. The Para Iwan-e-Dun (BWO) has it all," says Phil Iwane.

Phil Iwane can be found fishing with one of his Iwan-e-Duns frequently in the lower stretches of Cheesman Canyon. The Family Hole and Ice Box are known for big trout that are eager to feed on blue-winged olive imitations. Rainy or overcast days produce the best hatches as the high humidity stalls the development of the duns, keeping them on the water longer in comparison to bright and sunny days when they take flight immediately after emergence.

The design of the abdomen is what separates this fly from other parachute patterns. "I decided on using a piece of monofilament with the same thickness as the natural mayflies' abdomen. The monofilament has a natural curl that mimics a mayfly's abdomen. I flatten one end of the monofilament with a hemostat so that it doesn't roll when I tie it to the hook shank. For the tails, I use two dun-colored MicroFibbets instead of several rooster hackle fibers that most mayfly patterns incorporate into their design. To complete the abdomen, I use olive thread and palmer it over the monofilament." Iwane completes the extended body by coating it with UV resin to simulate the sheen of the naturals found streamside.

Iwane ties several different color variations of the Para Iwan-e-Dun, including PMD, Pink, Trico, and Adams. "The beauty of this pattern is that you can tie any mayfly using this technique by using a different-size monofilament and thread color based on the size and type of mayfly. You can tie a mayfly as large as a green drake or as small as a Trico." Iwane also ties a thorax-version (hackle is wrapped in the thorax area, then trimmed underneath) in a similar color scheme to mix up the profile and the way it floats on the water.

Iwane fishes his Iwan-e-Dun series as a single dry fly with a 9-foot 5X leader terminating in 5X to 7X tippet. He prefers a down-and-across presentation, with a reach cast, so that the fly proceeds the tippet and leader. Iwane recommends tying (or purchasing) his Iwan-e-Dun (BWO) in sizes 18 to 24 to be prepared for both the spring and autumn hatches. The spring "olives" are typically a size 18 or 20, and the autumn hatches are one to two sizes smaller. "Trout eat this fly with confidence. It floats high on the water and it is easy to see. The Iwane-e-Dun has truly become my go-to pattern when trout are feeding on mayfly duns."

- **Hook:** #16–#20 TMC 101
- **Thread:** Light-olive 8/0 Uni-Thread
- **Tail:** Whiting Coq de Leon fibers, light dun or light-speckled (4 or 5 fibers, 1½ x hook shank length, flared)
- **Abdomen:** Trouthunter PMD-colored stripped goose biot
- **Wing:** Hareline Clear Wing tied spent, 1½ body length
- **Thorax:** Trouthunter PMD-colored dry-fly dubbing
- **Hackle:** Whiting Farms light-dun saddle hackle, 2 wraps in back of wing and 1 wrap in front of wing. Clip top and bottom to allow fly to lay flat on water.

PMD Spinner

(Tied by Rick Yancik)

Rick Yancik is a true master when it comes to tying and fishing mayfly spinners. In addition to being a consummate angler, he is always willing to share his vast knowledge with others to help them elevate their dry-fly game to the next level. "Mayfly spinners represent the final stage in the life cycle of a mayfly. In some ways, mayfly spinners are often an overlooked and underrated stage of the mayfly life cycle. The importance of mayfly spinners to trout is not equal across all species of mayflies. For example, pale morning dun (PMD), Trico, and gray drake spinners usually occur in great abundance and contribute significantly to a trout's diet," Yancik explains.

Yancik thoroughly enjoys the challenges that are associated with PMD spinner falls. He is of the belief that the tougher it is to fool a difficult trout, the greater the reward. "To the angler who recognizes and understands the PMD spinner stage, fly fishing during a spinner fall can be both challenging and rewarding. Understanding the environmental conditions under which mating and a PMD spinner fall occurs is important. Wind, temperature, and precipitation play a significant

Rick Yancik's PMD Spinner fills an important niche when it comes to matching the hatch during the summer months. Many anglers overlook PMD spinner falls, which can be a huge oversight because they can provide some exceptional dry-fly opportunities. Spinner falls bring the best out of any serious dry-fly angler—but most of the time, the rewards are worth the effort.

role and influence both occurrence and intensity of a spinner fall. PMD spinner falls often occur under lower-light conditions typically observed later in the evening or early morning when the air temperature warms, winds are calmer, and precipitation is nonexistent or very light at best. A PMD spinner fall is often shortened or delayed due to nonoptimal environmental conditions such as wind and/or rain. This delay can result in the spinner fall occurring later into the evening or the following morning as the air warms. Spinner falls can also occur during the dun emergence stage, which is typically midmorning to early afternoon. Trout often will switch from feeding on duns to spinners, which are not going to leave the water. As such, it is important to observe the feeding behavior of trout."

Yancik's spinner imitations are works of art. He believes that tying PMD spinner imitations requires attention to a few simple details, which are relatively easy to mimic. "First, spinners, upon falling to the water, lie flat and exhibit little movement. After all, they are in the final stage of life, depositing their eggs and dying. Second, the bodies of spinners are typically thinner than the adult dun. This is the result of the dun shedding the skin in transitioning to the spinner stage. Third, spinner bodies tend to exhibit pronounced segmentation and often vary in color from adult duns. Fourth, tails are much more elongated than that of the adult dun, and upon falling onto the water are noticeably spent. And fifth, spinner wings are transparent or clear-like and are spent (lie flat) on the water. The combination of the above details translates into a "silhouette" on the surface in the eyes of trout below the surface. Wings and tails should be tied with sparseness in mind. Use only enough material to allow the spinner to lie flat in the film and not sink. Avoid bulkier wings, tails, and bodies except for cases of fishing fast water or fishing larger mayfly spinners such as gray and brown drakes. Because PMD spinners lie flat and their spent wings are transparent, they often appear invisible to the angler."

Yancik offers this advice on fishing spinners: "I prefer a downstream approach, casting across and down at an angle from 30 to 45 degrees. The exception being situations where visibility is more impaired or the backcast impeded. I tend to have more options for managing the length of the fly's drift and ensuring the fly always reaches the trout before the tippet/leader. I throw slack in the line as the fly falls to the water by a gentle lift of the rod tip and then lowering the rod, and sometimes using an air mend. I cast so the fly gently lands on the water like the natural and roughly 3 feet ahead of the trout I'm targeting. Upon a take (and the trout's take is a delicate sip), I gently lift the rod tip, and that is enough to set the hook."

Yancik offers this final thought: "One of the most important things in fly fishing is to watch the fish. They tell you most everything you need to know. Take time to observe and use this hindsight as foresight, and adjust accordingly . . . you'll be rewarded!"

PMD Spinner falls provide dry-fly enthusiasts with technical yet rewarding dry-fly fishing. Precise casting and delicate deliveries are a must in the glassy pools where you'll find selective trout feeding on spent-wing PMDs.

Poor Witch

(Tied by Pat Dorsey)

- **Hook:** #18–#24 Tiemco 101
- **Thread:** Gray 8/0 Uni-Thread
- **Tail:** Moose body hair
- **Abdomen:** Gray Superfine dubbing
- **Wings:** Blue dun hen hackle tied spent
- **Hackle:** Brown and grizzly rooster hackle

The legacy of Jim Poor began when he opened up Mountain View Tackle in the basement of a motel in Littleton, Colorado, in 1954. Poor's small tackle shop catered to both conventional and fly anglers alike. The staff at Anglers All shares this information pertaining to the evolution of their business. "In 1969 the City of Littleton relocated Mountain View Tackle in order to build Arapahoe Community College. With the new location just up the road, the name was changed to Anglers All. Anglers All is still in the same building today. Jim and his wife, Jane, continued to own and operate the store until the mid-1980s, when Bill Shappel and Terry Nicholson took the reigns." Bill Shappel retired and the Nicholsons were the sole owners until 2009, when Chris Keeley bought them out.

When I began fly fishing in the early 1970s, Anglers All was the only place in town where you could find a fly smaller than a size 18. Poor was arguably one of the best anglers and small-fly tiers of his time. A few of Poor's signature flies are featured in Jack Dennis's *Western Trout Fly Tying Manual* (Volume 2). According the Dennis, "Jim cut his teeth on

Jim Poor is a legend in Colorado. He was a pioneer in educating the masses on the importance of fishing with small flies. The Poor Witch is a pattern that every angler should carry in his or her fly box to imitate spent-wing mayflies.

the South Platte River south of Denver, which is considered by many to be one of the finest-quality fishing waters to be found today. This is a place where anglers can test their skill with very small dry flies, which at times may be as small as size #24 or even smaller. After being involved with the South Platte River for over 40 years, Jim's practical fishing experience with tiny fly patterns is unequaled."

Poor devoted his life to educating anglers and helping them elevate their skills to the next level. One of the greatest Trico patterns of all time is the Poor Witch, named after Jim Poor. The Poor Witch was designed to imitate a Trico spinner, which is the final stage of the hatch, when females come back to the water to lay their eggs. Spent-wing Tricos have a distinct silhouette that distinguishes their appearance from the duns. Anglers who fail to switch from upright-wing dun imitations to spent-wing patterns often become frustrated by their inability to catch fish. Unlike duns that leave the water quickly, dying spinners remain on the water for long periods of time. Trout take advantage of this opportunity and feed on Trico spinners voraciously.

Bob Saile, former outdoor editor at the *Denver Post*, was the first angler to show me the Poor Witch when we were fishing a Trico hatch together near Deckers. The Poor Witch was Saile's favorite Trico imitation because it fooled discerning trout that were feeding on the Trico spinners. In theory the Poor Witch is similar to a spent-wing Adams, but it has a forked tail composed of moose body hair, a thin abdomen dubbed from muskrat fur, and blue-dun hackle tips (instead of grizzly hen) with brown and grizzly rooster hackle (mixed) wrapped behind and in front of the wings.

Bill Shappel is extremely fond of the fly as well. "The Poor Witch is the best small (20–24) dry fly I have ever used, and my close fishing friends would agree. The Poor Witch is ideal for fooling trout feeding on Tricos, but it is also effective for other mayflies and midges as well." There's something special about the Poor Witch's silhouette, and the way it sits flush on the water's surface closely mimics the naturals. Unlike most Trico spinner imitations, the Poor Witch is easy to see, which is a distinct advantage when you are fishing with a size 24.

Trico hatches typically bring the wariest and craftiest trout to the surface to feed. They often require anglers to use long leaders (9–12 feet) terminating in spiderweb-thin 7X tippets. Precise yet delicate deliveries are a must for success. The best advice that I can give you is to get as close to the rising fish as possible—this usually means sneaking up on your hands and knees until you get into the desired casting location. Hands down the most effective tactic is making several repeated casts to a specific fish until the fish eats your fly. If you spook your target, you should have no problem finding another fish to cast to. Trico spinner falls typically last until 11:30 a.m. or so, then I take a break and enjoy some lunch after a wonderful morning of dry-fly fishing.

Trico hatches typically bring the wariest and craftiest fish to the surface because there are so many spent-wing mayflies on the water. Howard Stringert is a huge fan of a Poor Witch because he has fooled some really nice fish with it.

Purple Haze

(Tied by Greg Blessing)

- **Hook:** #14–#24 Tiemco 2487
- **Thread:** Black 8/0 Uni-Thread
- **Shuck:** Root Beer Krystal Flash
- **Abdomen:** Flashabou Weave or black, purple, and blue Flashabou, one strand each
- **Thorax:** Purple UV Ice Dub
- **Soft hackle:** Black Whiting Farms Herbert Miner Wet Fly Hackle

Greg Blessing and I have been friends for over 30 years. Blessing is the head guide at Angler's Covey in Colorado Springs, so he fishes the South Platte River several times a week. Our paths cross regularly, and we always make it a point to say hello to each other. I've always considered Blessing to be among the top industry professionals. In addition to being one of the state's best fly-fishing guides, he is an excellent fly tier. He's a tailwater enthusiast at heart and has designed a lot of proven patterns over the years to fool the finicky trout that reside throughout the entire South Platte watershed. One of his most popular flies is the Purple Haze.

Blessing first showed me his Purple Haze when we were fishing together in Eleven Mile Canyon. He had a fly box filled with them, so I knew it had to be one of his favorite patterns. After photographing his midge box, I could see why. The Purple Haze is a beautiful soft hackle with a lot of pizzazz.

I was intrigued about what inspired Blessing to come up with the Purple Haze. He told me this story: "The Purple Haze was a random thought. I was going down to Anglers Covey

Greg Blessing's Purple Haze is a nifty little soft hackle that works well when midges are hatching. Blessing is known for his trailing shuck patterns that incorporate a dash of flash into their design.

to buy some fly-tying materials to tie a blue soft hackle midge. Whenever I walk into a fly shop, I am always open-minded and looking for new fly-tying materials. That's when I stumbled upon Flashabou Weave. It's a unique material that combines three strands (black, purple, and blue) of Flashabou into one braid with unique flash properties. From every angle, the weave looks different, so I wanted to try this material for the abdomen on a soft hackle," Blessing explained.

Many of Blessing's patterns use a looped strand of Root Beer Krystal Flash for a trailing shuck. It provides a realistic silhouette and appearance, plus it adds a little extra flash. Blessing began the fly with his proven trailing shuck, then incorporated the Flashabou Weave into the fly's design for the abdomen. To build up the thorax, he added some Purple UV Ice Dub, then completed the fly with three wraps of black Whiting Farms Herbert Miner Wet Fly Hackle (hen) to simulate the wings and legs of the emerging adult.

At this juncture, this fly did not have a name; it was soft hackle that was a work in progress. "I went fishing at Deckers with Chris Ramos, a colleague of mine, and started in Ray's Run.

Greg Blessing's Purple Haze is a proven producer along the entire South Platte watershed. It can be fished underneath a strike indicator or fished like a traditional wet fly.

I began at the top of the run, swinging my soft hackle midge pattern through the current, and I caught several fish. After bringing several fish to hand, the soft hackle was becoming torn and tattered, and that's when I noticed that the blue Flashabou had gotten chewed off and the purple was more prominent. It was crazy—I started catching more fish with the purple color. Ramos asked me if I had changed flies. I told him what happened and we both laughed." After that outing, Blessing referred to his soft hackle as the Purple Haze.

Blessing tied up a bunch of Purple Hazes and started sharing them with his friends. They enjoyed similar success and asked for more. Two years later Perk Perkins (CEO of the Orvis Company) was in town for a business meeting and needed to borrow some equipment and flies to fish in Eleven Mile Canyon! Mike Clough, Rocky Mountain Regional Business Manager for Orvis, accompanied him. "I gave them a bunch of Purple Hazes and they did very well with them. Mr. Perkins asked me if Orvis could add it to their fly inventory via their royalty program, and Clough helped initiate the process to get the Purple Haze into the Orvis catalog."

At that point the fly started getting some national recognition. Orvis was tying the Purple Haze in larger sizes, and it quickly became a popular soft hackle for imitating caddis. "The next time I was on the Big Horn River, I started swinging a size 14 Purple Haze and caught a bunch of fish at the Cliff Hole. It was a sight to see."

Blessing's Purple Haze is extremely versatile—it can be dead-drifted underneath a strike indicator with a conventional tandem nymphing rig, or you can employ traditional soft hackle tactics. The Purple Haze is effective in faster riffles, particularity near mid-channel shelves that drop off into a pool or tailout.

Puterbaugh Caddis

(Tied by Don Puterbaugh)

- **Hook:** #14–#18 Tiemco 100
- **Thread:** Black 6/0 Uni-Thread
- **Abdomen:** 1.5–2 mm black closed-cell foam
- **Wing:** Natural elk
- **Hackle:** Whiting Farms brown rooster

If you've spent any length of time in Colorado, you are probably aware of the famed Mother's Day caddis hatch on the Arkansas River. The blizzard-like hatch begins toward the latter part of April and extends until the middle part of May. Spring runoff is often the deciding factor on the duration of the hatch. Dry-fly enthusiasts typically find reliable surface action until the river blows out from snowmelt. Once the high-water season subsides, sporadic caddis continue to play an important role throughout the remainder of the summer months.

Don Puterbaugh, a longtime resident of Salida, Colorado, is credited with designing the Puterbaugh Caddis. Puterbaugh is a legend in the Arkansas Valley, having spent upwards of 250 days a year on the water each season during the height of his career, guiding clients, teaching schools, as well as enjoying some personal time on the river. Puterbaugh is also the author of several

The Puterbaugh Caddis has been a favorite in the Arkansas Valley for over 50 years. It won't take you long to figure out why—the Puterbaugh Caddis is easy to tie, durable, extremely visible, and floats high on western freestones. I've been blessed to spend several days on the Arkansas River with Puterbaugh, learning from the master himself. Each day with Puterbaugh was filled with many valuable lessons that I'll treasure for a lifetime.

fly-tying books and a royalty tier for Umpqua Feather Merchants.

Puterbaugh designed his caddis pattern in 1964, with the primary objective of creating a fly that was simple to tie, floated well, and was easy to see. The Puterbaugh Caddis is constructed from closed-cell foam, so it floats like a cork. Puterbaugh recommends using 2 mm foam for a size 14 and 1.5 mm foam for sizes 16 to 18. "I'm a firm believer in a wing you can see! That's why I tie this pattern with a light bull-elk wing, but not bleached, because it is too brittle. The elk wing also assists in higher floatation," says Puterbaugh.

Success during a caddis hatch begins by being in the right place at the right time. The water farthest from the source (snowfields) in lower elevations begins to warm first, and that's precisely where you'll find the first caddisflies. When the river's temperature reaches 54 degrees in a particular location, caddis begin emerging. It makes complete sense that you'll find 54-degree water temperature in Canon City earlier than Salida, earlier in Hecla Junction in comparison to Buena Vista, and so on. Being on the leading edge of the hatch is critical for success. I strongly recommend contacting a local fly shop for detailed information on the exact location of the hatch. If you're fishing where the caddisflies' concentration is the heaviest, your odds of finding feeding trout go way down because they are jam-packed with both pupae and adults. If you're on the front edge of the hatch, the fishing is usually exceptional.

It's not uncommon to experience a cold snap in April or May, or possibly get some snow, which can stall the hatch until the water warms back up again. Don't fret: There can be some excellent blue-winged olive hatches under these conditions, especially when the skies are overcast. During inclement weather the dry-fly fishing can be epic with "olive" imitations. Make sure your fly boxes are crammed with plenty of Mathew's Sparkle Duns and Cannon's Snowshoe Duns in a size 20.

Puterbaugh recommends using a paste floatant on the elk wing but not on the foam abdomen. He believes that putting floatant on the foam adds weight and compromises its floatability. A combination of tactics works well when fishing with caddis adults. If you are not getting the results you hoped for by dead-drifting a Puterbaugh Caddis, try skating or skittering it, as this usually entices an aggressive take. This tactic is effective when the ovipositing females return to the water during the low-light hours. Another trick that works well during a blanket hatch, especially when you are having trouble deciphering your fly from the naturals on the water, is upsizing your imitation by one hook size.

Don Puterbaugh passed away on May 29, 2021. I was extremely fortunate to have had a nice phone conversation with him during the summer of 2020 and to get him to tie the fly you see pictured at the beginning of this chapter. Don, I am forever grateful for our river time and your contribution to this project.

With Greg Felt at the oars, Kim Dorsey pounds the stream banks in Brown's Canyon with a Puterbaugh Caddis. The Puterbaugh Caddis is a great choice during the summer months, as opportunistic trout waste little time eating them.

Red Quill Parachute

(Tied by A. K. Best)

- **Hook:** #14–#18 Tiemco 100
- **Thread:** Rusty-brown 6/0 Danville
- **Tail:** Brown hackle fibers
- **Abdomen:** Dyed brown quill from a turkey flat
- **Wing:** White turkey flat
- **Thorax:** Tan Superfine
- **Hackle:** Whiting Farms brown rooster hackle

A. K. Best is in a league of his own when it comes to tying tiny dry flies. Best is a resident of Boulder, Colorado, but he is nationally known for his craft and attention to detail. Best is the author of four books that should be in every serious fly tier's library: *Production Fly Tying*, *Dyeing and Bleaching Natural Fly-Tying Materials*, *A. K.'s Fly Box*, and *Fly Fishing with A.K.* In *A.K's Fly Box* John Gierach sums it up best in the introduction: "The mark A. K. puts on fly patterns is easier to see than it is to describe. The first thing you'll notice about his flies is that they're beautifully tied: neat, crisp, and elegant. His dry flies especially

have a realistic, delicate look—although when you fish them, you'll notice that they're surprisingly durable."

A. K.'s Red Quill Parachute has long been a favorite for the *Rhithrogena undulata*, or small western red quill, which begins hatching in mid-August and extends into the middle part of September. Red quills, as they are commonly called, fill an important void between the midsummer mayflies (pale morning duns and green drakes) and the autumn bluewinged olives. In many watersheds throughout Colorado, red quills are a game-changer during the dog days of summer, when fishing

A. K. Best's flies are true works of art. His Red Quill Parachute is a great choice on the Frying Pan, Williams Fork, Arkansas, and Colorado Rivers when red quills emerge in late summer and early fall.

becomes slow from receding river levels, warm water temperatures, and sporadic hatches.

In *A. K's Fly Box*, Best offers this advice: "The Red Quill is a fly you should have in your fly box at all times in a wide range of sizes. A Red Quill Parachute is an excellent option when there is no hatch but you don't feel like sitting on the bank for an hour or two waiting for one to begin. I have caught a lot of nice trout at times like that. Evidently, they didn't want to wait an hour or two either. I have found the Red Quill pattern very effective from as early as late May to as late as early October. If you were to limit your fly selection to only a few patterns, you would be wise to include the Red Quill."

I cannot live without this fly in August and September—it's truly one of my top-producing dry flies. Anglers can find reliable red quill hatches on several of Colorado's tailwaters. One of my favorite tailraces to find red quills hatching is on the Williams Fork River, below

The autumn red quill hatches on the Williams Fork River are something to talk about. Scores of rising fish eat the mahogany-colored duns each evening in September, capping off a great day in Middle Park. Savvy anglers like Doug McElveen mark this hatch in their calendar and make it a point to partake in the festivities each season.

Williams Fork Reservoir. It's a late-afternoon/evening event—the duns typically begin hatching around 4:30 p.m. and continue until 6 p.m. The Colorado River is in close proximity and has a similar hatch that attracts savvy dry-fly enthusiasts as well.

Parachute patterns have a distinct advantage in foam lines and harsh glare where others flies are difficult to see. A parachute-style fly has the hackle wrapped horizontally around the wing (oftentimes referred to as the post), rather than wound vertically around the shank of the hook. Parachute patterns have the same goal in mind as a No Hackle or Comparadun, allowing the body to sit lower in the surface film, providing a more realistic impression to the fish. The upright wing produces the important silhouette that dun imitations require, but furthermore, the wing makes the fly much easier to see and follow on the water. "I substituted white T-base for the wing post because the feathers are lighter than calf hair. White T-base is the feather found on the neck and breast of the bird and is only 2 to 3 inches long. This allows me to tie a slightly taller wing for visibility. The quill body is made from stripped and dyed white turkey flat quill. Two turns of hackle are all that's needed for an 18. I use three turns for a 14 and 16."

During the height of a red quill hatch, it is important to pick out one surface-feeder and cast to that specific fish. It is important to start in the back of a run or pool, casting to the closest feeding fish and systematically working your way toward the head end of the run. If your Red Quill Parachute begins to sink, Best offers this helpful advice: "Don't use a white powder (I call it fairy dust) in an attempt to remove fish slime after you have landed a fish. It doesn't remove slime, it dehydrates it." Best recommends several crisp false casts to shake the water off the fly and reapplying a paste floatant to keep it afloat.

Rojo Midge

(Tied by Greg Garcia)

- **Hook:** #18–#22 Tiemco 200R
- **Gills:** Oral-B dental floss
- **Bead:** Ruby Killer Caddis silver lined glass (extra small)
- **Thread:** Red Ultra Thread 70 denier
- **Rib:** Red UTC Ultra Wire (extra small)
- **Collar:** Dyed bright-green peacock herl

Midge larvae that reside in the substrate of a stream or lake with low oxygen levels are often referred as bloodworms, blood midges, or red larvae. These larvae are bright red because they contain hemoglobin, the same oxygen-carrying pigment that makes our blood red. Oftentimes midge larvae are overlooked as an important food source because they don't appear to be as prevalent as pupae and adults. The "out of sight, out of mind" mentality can be a huge oversight, however, as my research indicates that larval densities in healthy, weed-rich substrates may range between 800 and 2,000 midge larvae per square meter.

You would be hard-pressed to find a better blood midge imitation than Greg Garcia's Rojo Midge. It has been a Colorado favorite for years because it consistently fools fish under a wide range of conditions. "I first started tinkering with the Rojo Midge in 1997. Like most of my flies, they remain in my fly box for years and undergo changes along the way. I have always felt like it takes time for them to evolve into a proven pattern. After 6 years of tweaking the design, I submitted the Rojo Midge to

Greg Garcia's Rojo Midge is indispensable if you plan on fishing one of Colorado's fabled tailwaters or legendary stillwater impoundments. Garcia's design incorporates a thin and sparse red wormlike abdomen (as the name implies) with a peacock herl collar and pronounced gills that simulate life. The end result is a pattern that fools selective trout wherever they swim.

Umpqua Feather Merchants for their catalog. In 2004 it went into production and became available at specialty fly shops throughout the country," he explained.

Garcia first tied the Rojo Midge on a Tiemco 100, but later switched to a 200R because the longer hook shank produced a better worm-like appearance. Garcia uses Oral-B dental floss for the gills but admits he experimented with other materials. "At first I tried Antron, Z-Lon, and Poly Yarn. All these materials were too stiff and didn't move well." The gills are tied near the front of the hook, protruding forward over the hook eye. Once the gills are tied in place, Garcia slides a ruby extra-small Killer Caddis Bead over the tie-in point of the gills snug to the eye of the hook.

The original pattern calls for red Ultra Thread 70 denier, but Garcia also recommends tying this pattern in black, olive, and purple. Garcia offers this advice for tying the abdomen: "I like the sheen that the Ultra Thread has. It also lays down flat, like wrapping floss. I spin the bobbin counterclockwise to keep the thread smooth and uniform. If you are left-handed, spin your bobbin clockwise."

Segmentation is an important part of designing a midge larva or pupa. Garcia uses extra-small Ultra Wire to create a wormlike appearance. "I use red on red, copper on black, chartreuse on olive, and turquoise on purple. Ribbing is a critical part of the flies' design because it represents the segmentation of the natural." The final step is tying a collar out of peacock herl behind the bead. Peacock herl has a natural translucence that attracts fish. Garica likes to use peacock that is dyed bright green.

The most effective way to fish a Rojo Midge is on the dead drift underneath a strike indicator. "To be proficient at nymph fishing, I believe two things have to come into play: First you have to present your flies at the right speed and depth, and second, you have to have confidence in your rig and tactics." Garcia recommends using a 7½-foot nylon tapered leader terminating in 5X. Off the end of the leader, he ties on a piece of 5X fluorocarbon tippet (12–14 inches long) where he attaches his first fly. The Rojo Midge, particularly red, is an excellent attractor in a tandem nymph rig. Off the Rojo Midge, Garcia adds an additional 12 to 14 inches of 6X fluorocarbon tippet, then attaches a dropper-fly to match any visible hatches. For instance, if blue-winged olives are hatching, trail a *Baetis* nymph; if there are midges emerging, trail a midge pupa; and so on.

Garcia is a big fan of using a piece of polypropylene yarn for a strike indicator and some weight (split shot or a putty alternative) directly above the knot that joins the tippet and leader together. "I place the yarn indicator two times the depth of the water I'm fishing. This is easy to figure out . . . if I am fishing in 3 feet of water, I place my yarn 6 feet up from my bottom fly."

Garcia's Rojo Midge is a proven favorite among anglers that frequent the Deckers area. During the winter a red Rojo Midge is an excellent attractor in a tandem nymphing rig, especially in the slower pools and tailouts where the heaviest concentration of fish are found. FORREST DORSEY

RS 2

(Tied by Rim Chung)

- **Hook:** #16–#24
  Tiemco 101
- **Thread:** Gray 8/0
  Uni-Thread
- **Tail:** Two medium-dun
  MicroFibbets
- **Abdomen:** Natural
  beaver fur
- **Wing:** Gray saddle
  hackle webbing

Rim Chung invented the original RS 2 back in the early 1970s. RS 2 stands for Rim's Semblance, number 2. It's predecessor, the RS 1, had a wing case instead of an emerging wing. Chung's objective for designing the RS 2 was to come up with a simple yet realistic nymph that imitated an emerging mayfly. Chung's original recipe included a straight-eye hook, two moose body fibers for the tail, natural beaver fur for the abdomen, and the webbing off a gray saddle hackle feather (the fluffy material near the stem) for the emerging wing. Chung's latest version uses two medium-dun MicroFibbets for the tail instead of the moose body fibers.

Modern-day innovation has led to several variations of the original pattern including the Sparkle Wing RS 2, Flashback RS 2, Mercury RS 2, Mercury Flashback RS 2, and a Foam Wing RS 2. The Sparkle Wing RS 2 was developed by Blue Quill Angler guide Bob Churchill, whereby he substituted Metallic Opal Ribbon Floss for the wing instead of using the gray saddle hackle webbing. Churchill also tweaked the tail and used elk-hair fibers instead of Micro-Fibbets, giving it a unique flavor of its own.

The RS 2 is arguably one of the best trout patterns of all time. It has fooled countless trout along the South Platte corridor—from the headwaters to the outskirts of Denver. The most important attribute to a well-tied RS 2 is keeping it thin and sparse, as bulky imitations do not perform as well.

The Flashback RS 2 was invented by Roaring Fork and South Platte River guide Tom Whitley. His design incorporated a split, MicroFibbet tail (clipped), Adams gray Superfine dubbing for the abdomen, pearl Mylar tinsel for the flashback, and white ostrich herl for the wing. I tweaked Whitley's pattern and came up with my own variation—the Mercury Flashback RS 2. My pattern uses dun hackle fibers for the tail (for the ease of tying), gray or olive Superfine dubbing for a thin and sparse abdomen, Prism White Glamour Madera for the wing, and a small silver-lined glass bead to enhance the gas-bubble effect that occurs during the emerging process.

The Foam Wing RS 2, commonly referred to as Foam Wing Emerger, was invented by San Juan River Guide John Tavenner and has become a staple throughout Colorado. His variation is tied in both gray and brown. He uses brown rooster for the tail, a thread abdomen, 2 mm white craft foam for the wing, and Superfine dubbing (gray or brown to match the tying thread) for the thorax.

Wendy Kanable enjoys a beautiful autumn day on the Williams Fork River during the last week of September. Bluebird days do not typically produce reliable dry-fly fishing, but the nymphing can be exceptional with patterns like a RS 2 that imitate emerging blue-winged olives.

Although gray and brown seem to be the colors of choice, you can change the color of the thread and dubbing to match just about any mayfly hatch. For instance, use PMD Superfine for a PMD emerger or BWO Superfine to imitate a blue-winged olive emerger, and so on. In smaller sizes, such as a #24, a black RS 2 works well for Tricos and midge emergers.

According to Chung, "The RS 2 is an emerger, but it shouldn't be treated as a traditional emerger. It shouldn't be limited to near-surface fishing, but rather fished in a classical ascending manner. This fly should be fished as a nymph." The vast majority of anglers fish an RS 2 underneath a strike indicator in a tandem nymphing rig. I typically trail an RS 2 off an attractor like a San Juan Worm, UV Scud, Pat's Rubber Legs, crane-fly larva, or a leech.

It never hurts to think outside the box from time to time and use the greased-leader technique when you think trout are feeding on emergers. Identifying a headless head-to-tail rise is the telltale sign trout are keying on emergers. Ed Engle explains it best in his book *Fishing Small Flies.* "It is critically important to determine whether a head-to-tail riser is taking from just below the surface or on top. If the trout are keying on emergers near the surface, you'll see mostly the back of the fish behind the head, the dorsal fin, and the tail. The head itself will be conspicuously invisible. I call it the headless head-to tail rise."

To incorporate the greased-leader tactic into your bag of tricks, apply dry-fly floatant to the entire leader except the last 12 inches closest to the fly. This allows your fly to sit just below the surface film precisely where you would find emerging duns. Locating your fly is the greatest challenge when fishing emergers—anglers need to have a keen eye—and set the hook to any rising trout near your fly.

Slim Shady 5.0

(Tied by Juan Ramirez)

- **Hook:** #16–#20 Daichii 1270
- **Thread:** Light-brown 8/0 Uni-Thread
- **Tail:** Black MicroFibbets, split
- **Rib:** Brown, Hopper Juan's Slim Rib
- **Thorax:** Light-brown 8/0 Uni-Thread
- **Wing case:** Black holographic tinsel (medium)
- **Legs:** Black Fluoro Fibre (12 strands)
- **Wing case resin:** Deer Creek Diamond Fine

Whether you're fishing on one of Colorado's illustrious freestones or its renowned tailwaters, you'll need a thorough selection of *Baetis* nymphs. Blue-winged olives, commonly referred to as *Baetis*, are the first mayflies to hatch in the spring and the last to emerge in the fall. *Baetis* nymphs can be identified by their forked tail, slim, dark-olive abdomen, and prominent wing pad. Prior to emergence their wing pads become unusually dark and swollen, which is a sure sign they are ready to emerge into an adult.

Baetis are multibrooded, which adds a small twist into the equation, as each following generation is smaller than the previous one. This means the "olives" that hatch in the spring are one or two sizes larger than those found emerging in the fall, so you'll need to make the necessary adjustments.

There are a lot of different *Baetis* nymphs to choose from, but Juan Ramirez's Slim Shady

Juan Ramirez's Slim Shady 5.0 is the perfect imposter to imitate a Baetis *nymph.* Baetis *nymphs are available to opportunistic trout year-round, but their greatest importance is during the height of a blue-winged olive emergence. Spring hatches typically begin in late March and last through mid-May. Autumn emergences occur toward the latter part of August and continue to be an important part of matching the hatch through mid-November.*

5.0 is on the top of the list for most anglers in Colorado. "The Slim Shady 5.0 is tied on a Daiichi 1270 hook. I chose that particular hook model because it is 3X long, which gives it a traditional mayfly nymph look. As the name implies, it's a slim pattern that closely mimics several of the smaller mayflies you'll encounter in the southern Rockies," says Juan Ramirez.

The Slim Shady 5.0 is a pattern that Ramirez worked on for several years before he finally found the right material to set it apart from other great patterns. "It took several versions, but I finally settled on a design that utilized a 'secret' material called Slim Rib. It's a micro stretch material that I use to make realistic segmentation on my mayfly nymphs. No one else is using this material, and that's what sets this pattern apart from all the other mayfly nymphs out there."

Ramirez puts the finishing touch on his pattern with some black holographic tinsel for the wing case and black Fluoro Fibre to imitate the legs. He applies some UV resin on the black holographic tinsel to give it that "bursting at the seams" look prior to emergence. Ramirez further tweaks the shade of his mayfly nymphs by adjusting the color scheme of the tying thread to match specific hatches. His favorite thread choices are light brown, tobacco, cinnamon, tan, and olive dun. Ramirez is particularly fond of light brown or olive dun for *Baetis* nymphs, but finds tan works well for a PMD nymph by upsizing his imitation. He also finds the larger sizes to be effective for imitating Yellow Sally nymphs.

Ramirez has rigorously tested the Slim Shady 5.0 on several of the state's renowned tailwaters and storied freestones, and the end result is a pattern that consistently fools finicky trout just about anywhere you fish. It is one of his go-to patterns when he is guiding or enjoying a personal day on the stream.

Ramirez recommends fishing the Slim Shady with a conventional two- or three-fly tandem nymphing rig. His favorite time of the year to fish his Slim Shady 5.0 is during the shoulder seasons and midsummer months when the heaviest concentrations of nymphs are on the move. "Some of my favorite sight-fishing moments have been when the fish are keyed on either emerging *Baetis* nymphs or pale morning dun nymphs near the surface. The trout line up and pick off the emergers like low-hanging fruit."

During the height of a blue-winged olive hatch, Ramirez likes to use a split-back version. "As the nymphs prepare to split the thorax (emerge) and transform into an adult, the split-back variation duplicates this stage precisely." The split-back variation uses gray or dark-gray razor foam for the wing case, overlaid with medium black holographic tinsel along the edges. The small strip of exposed razor foam imitates the mayfly's wing splitting through the thorax area prior to emergence.

Savvy anglers like Robbie Jardine know the importance of fishing with Baetis *nymphs during the spring season. Juan Ramirez's Slim Shady 5.0 is a great option when you begin to see trout feeding on mayfly nymphs in shallow riffles or transitional zones.*

Snowshoe Dun

(Tied by Jim Cannon)

- **Hook:** #16–#14 Tiemco 101
- **Thread:** Olive 6/0 Danville
- **Tail:** Dun MicroFibbets
- **Body:** Olive 6/0 Danville
- **Wing:** Snowshoe rabbit foot hair

Jim Cannon, a longtime resident of Evergreen, Colorado, and former owner of the Blue Quill Angler, originated the Snowshoe Dun back in the early 1990s, but he is quick to give credit to two well-known fly tiers—Adirondack legend Francis Betters and Denver-based fly designer John Betts—for influencing his design. If you're a fan of low riders or Comparadun-type dry flies, Jim Cannon's Snowshoe Dun will quickly earn a spot in your fly box.

According to Cannon, "The Snowshoe Dun is both realistic and impressionistic at the same time. The tail is tied sparse with four synthetic tailing fibers (two on each side), which helps stabilize the fly, keeping it upright and floating flush in the surface film. The tailing material was first introduced by John Betts, a pioneer in the use of synthetic materials during the 1970s. Betts is known for using products like Tyvek, Zing Wing, nylon organza, and Z-Lon in his fly designs."

The Snowshoe Dun's tapered abdomen is made from 6/0 thread. Cannon changes the color of the thread based on the species of mayfly he is trying to imitate. For instance, for blue-winged olives, he likes using Danville #60

Jim Cannon's Snowshoe Dun has fooled super-selective surface feeders all over the state of Colorado. Whether you are fishing on one of the state's fabled freestones like the Arkansas, Roaring Fork, Eagle, Gunnison, Colorado, and so on, or a smooth, flowing gin-clear tailwater like the South Platte, Taylor, or Frying Pan River, Cannon's Snowshoe Dun is essential for matching the hatch.

olive thread. Cannon advises, "The color for PMDs can be anywhere from yellow, ginger, or light olive to pink, depending on the stream and species. You'll need to tweak the color of the thread abdomen to match the naturals on your favorite stream." Cannon uses the same concept for his Trico Snowshoe Dun by using the appropriate colored thread for the abdomen. Cannon ties black and olive abdomens to imitate both the male and female Tricos.

Dry-fly enthusiasts refer to blue-winged olives, pale morning duns, and Tricos as the "Big Three" when discussing mayflies. This grouping of mayflies produces reliable dry-fly fishing between late March and mid-November. Cannon also ties a larger variety of his Snowshoe Dun to imitate western green drakes, which is the largest mayfly to hatch in Colorado. The drake hatch typically occurs in late June and extends into the middle part of July in most watersheds. It's not uncommon to see some sporadic hatches lasting into the month of August on some of Colorado's tailwaters.

Cannon is a firm believer in tying his Snowshoe Dun thin and sparse. Cannon advises tiers to use a few fibers of dubbing for the

The shoulder seasons provide dry-fly enthusiasts like Jim Cannon with plenty of opportunities to catch trout with surface offerings. One of Cannon's go-to patterns during the onset of fall is his Snowshoe Dun (BWO).

thorax, which aids in holding the wing in place. "The slightly larger thorax area of the fly is made from Fine & Dry dubbing but can also be made from natural rabbit fur or beaver with the guard hairs removed. Whatever material is used, it should be used sparingly to just build up around the wing and thorax area."

The wing is what separates this pattern from others like it. "The wing is composed from a blend of snowshoe rabbit foot hair. The hair from the feet of the snowshoe rabbit has been used in tying flies for at least half a century. My research indicates that Francis Betters first used snowshoe rabbit to tie a caddisfly imitation. Betters was looking for a buoyant material that would allow him to pull the fly underwater and then have it pop up like an emerging caddis pupae. Since the hair off the foot of the snowshoe rabbit is composed of thousands of kinks, it contains the unique properties of buoyancy by trapping air in the follicles. Just as the insulating properties of the hair protect the feet of the snowshoe rabbit all winter long as it sits on ice and snow, when tied on a hook, it traps air, making the fly extremely buoyant."

Cannon recommends using a 9- or 12-foot tapered leader when fishing a Snowshoe Dun. "Make sure you use dry-fly crystals for your floatant instead of paste alternatives. Paste floatants mat down the snowshoe rabbit fibers, causing the fly to sink."

The Snowshoe Dun is most often fished on the dead drift, either upstream, downstream, up and across, or down and across. On occasion, I'll skitter Cannon's Snowshoe Green Drake, as it mimics the naturals struggling to get off the water. Due to their size, green drakes take considerably longer to escape the water's surface and take flight. Oftentimes, they skitter before flying off the water's surface, which draws attention to them, triggering an aggressive riseform.

South Platte Brassie

(Tied by Pat Dorsey)

- **Hook:** #18–#24 Tiemco 101
- **Thread:** Gray 8/0 Uni-Thread
- **Abdomen:** Copper UTC wire (small)
- **Thorax:** Gray Superfine

Gene Lynch, Ken Chandler, and Tug Davenport carved their way into angling history by inventing the South Platte Brassie back in the early 1960s. The Brassie was a group effort that originated during one of their routine tying sessions, when they came up with the idea of wrapping copper wire around a hook shank to provide additional weight and achieve a quicker sink rate to some of their favorite nymphs. This might sound a bit silly now, but keep in mind this was back in the 1960s, when all the modern-day advancements (e.g., bead heads, tungsten underbodies, and so on) were not available for fly tiers.

According to Bill Chandler, Ken Chandler's son, the invention of the South Platte Brassie was really an accident: One of their weighted nymphs came apart after fooling several fish on it, but to their surprise, the exposed copper wire underbody kept catching fish. With that concept in mind, Lynch, Chandler, and Davenport decided to use one of their copper wire underbodies and add a small piece of black heat shrink tubing for the head, a

The South Platte Brassie is an "oldie but a goodie" that has withstood the test of time. The "Brassie," as it is commonly referred to, works well during the height of a midge hatch, when trout are focused on eating pupae. The term "Brassie" came from the original pattern being tied from brass-plated copper wire from a transformer.

new concoction they began referring to as the South Platte Brassie.

In *Tying Small Flies* (Stackpole Books), Ed Engle states, "As the word got around about the effectiveness of the Brassie, innovative tiers began using enameled wire stripped from old motors, armatures, and transformers." There was one setback though. "Tiers who cranked out a season's supply over the winter found the bright, shiny copper wire oxidized within a month or so, and the flies became ineffective."

This is no longer a problem, as you can purchase spooled wire from any fly shop across the country. My favorite is Wapsi's Ultra Wire, a copper-based wire that is ideal for weight, ribbing, or bodies like the Brassie or John Barr's famous Copper John. Ultra Wire does not have a shelf life—it remains as shiny as the day it was purchased and is available in a wide variety of colors, including copper, red, black, blue, chartreuse, and olive. I tie my South Platte Brassies in all the previously mentioned colors because they all have a

The South Platte Brassie is a great option during the height of a midge hatch, especially during the winter months when trout key heavily on pupae. When a midge hatch becomes evident, swap out your larvae imitations for pupae imitations and fish them mid-column.

time and place when they are effective. A red Brassie is a nifty little blood midge imitation, a blue Brassie works well in low light, a copper Brassie is a deadly pupa imitation during the height of a midge hatch, and so on.

Fly tiers have taken the liberty to use different materials for the head, including gray or black dubbing, peacock herl, or a few wraps of black tying thread. Several years ago I opted to add a silver-lined glass bead to the original pattern and swap out the gray Superfine dubbing for peacock herl. I refer to this variation as the Mercury Brassie.

The Brassie is still among some of the top-producing fly patterns on the South Platte River, both in Cheesman Canyon and the nearby Deckers stretch. The Brassie is extremely versatile—it can be used in a tandem nymphing rig or used as a dropper off a dry fly. Sometimes I use the Brassie as an attractor and trail two flies behind it, particularly when I am looking for a dash of flash to draw attention to my dropper fly. During the height of a midge hatch, I like using a Brassie as my trailer, keeping it higher in the water column, where the greatest concentrations of midge pupae are found.

A Brassie is the perfect dropper off a dry fly, especially in shallow water, where traditional nymphing rigs get hung up or fish become suspicious or spooked by strike indicators. I typically drop a Brassie off a Stimulator, Amy's Ant, Elk Hair Caddis, or another buoyant dry fly with 18 to 24 inches of 6X tippet material.

Stalcup's Baetis

(Tied by Solitude Fly Company)

- **Hook:** #20–#22 Tiemco 200 R
- **Thread:** 6/0 olive Danville #60
- **Tail:** Partridge
- **Abdomen:** Olive D-Rib
- **Wing case:** Olive Medallion Sheeting
- **Legs:** Partridge
- **Thorax:** Olive Fine & Dry Dubbing

Shane Stalcup is considered by many to be one of the most innovative fly tiers of our time. Unfortunately, Stalcup's life was cut short when he passed away at the early age of 48 (May 11, 2011), but he left a long-lasting impression on the fly-fishing world. For over 30 years Stalcup tied flies commercially, supplying anglers around the globe with his realistic flies. As a commercial tier, I completely understand the discipline and commitment it takes to stay at home and tie seventy-five to one hundred dozen flies per week. Stalcup's efforts were truly remarkable and did not go unnoticed by the angling community.

If you don't have a copy of Stalcup's book *Mayflies "Top to Bottom"* (Frank Amato, 2002) in your library, you should purchase one. There is an entire section dedicated to tying his *Baetis* nymph with step-by-step tutorials on how to tie the fly. In the text Stalcup explains, "Of all the small mayfly nymphs I've tied over the years, this one has become my go-to fly."

Stalcup's Baetis uses partridge for the tail and olive D-Rib for the abdomen. Stalcup

It's hard to go wrong with a Stalcup's Baetis during the shoulder seasons when trout are feeding heavily on Baetis *nymphs. Having an imposter with the correct size, shape, and color is critical when matching the hatch. Stalcup's Baetis meets all of these criteria.*

recommends cutting the D-Rib at an angle to minimize bulk at the tie-in point. It's important to make sure that when you wrap the D-Rib forward around the hook shank, the curved side is facing up. Stalcup offers this solid advice in his book: "The first several wraps should be made with the tubing under a lot of tension. As you progress up the hook shank, relax the tension a little, until you get to the stopping point where you do not want any tension at all. This will create a tapered body that is translucent and segmented."

Stalcup's innovation spawned several new fly-tying materials that were available in his mail-order catalog. One of his most popular products was Medallion Sheeting, which is used for the wing case on his *Baetis* nymph. If you're not familiar with Medallion Sheeting, Stalcup sums it up nicely: "This synthetic wing material is a takeoff from Zing Wing; it is slightly thicker and has permanent color. It is very strong crossways, but it will tear lengthways. Although it was designed for wings,

Medallion Sheeting has become indispensable when it comes to tying nymphs. This stuff is great for wing cases. When used in this fashion, you get a wet and glistening wing case that is very lifelike."

Stalcup uses a somewhat different technique for the wing case, legs (partridge), and dubbed thorax. He explains this important information in his book: "On most flies, the wing case is tied in before the thorax is formed and then pulled over the top. On this fly, the wing case is tied in at the hook eye, extending out over it. By doing it this way, the legs can be tied in the middle of the thorax, making it look more natural. When the wing case is pulled back, the legs will splay out into two equal groups and sweep backwards." The final step is to secure the Medallion Sheeting with several wraps of thread behind the legs, then pull the thread under the body up to the eye of the hook, and whip-finish. When trimming the Medallion Sheeting, leave a little tag end. Clip a V in the tag end of the wing case to complete the fly.

The most effective method to fish your Stalcup's Baetis is with a conventional nymphing rig under a strike indicator. During the height of the hatch, make sure you are fishing it mid-column and allow it to swing in the current. *Baetis* nymphs are excellent swimmers, so trout routinely key on the uplifting behavior during emergence. If this pattern isn't one of your go-to *Baetis* nymphs now, it will be soon! I hope you enjoy this pattern as much as I have over the years.

This Cheesman Canyon brown trout fell for a size 22 Stalcup's Baetis during an afternoon blue-winged olive emergence. Switching from midge imitations to mayfly nymphs midday is a good strategy during the spring and fall months, when trout key heavily on Baetis *between noon and 3 p.m.* FORREST DORSEY

- **Hook:** #12–#16 Daiichi 1770
- **Thread:** Light-olive 70 Denier UTC
- **Body:** Light-green sewing thread
- **Dorsal strip:** Light-olive Swiss Straw
- **Rib:** Light-green sewing thread
- **Thorax:** Olive Ice Dub
- **Wing case:** Light-olive Swiss Straw
- **Eyes:** 25-pound mono (burnt) and 2 olive glass beads

Static Damsel

(Tied by Rick Takahashi)

Nothing excites a stillwater angler more than the words "ice-off." Lower-elevation lakes unthaw first (as early as March), but higher altitudes prolong ice-off until mid- to late April, or well into the summer months in the high country. "I look forward to spring, as the waters open up and the bugs start to stir the interest of feeding trout, especially the emergence of the damsels from nymphs to the winged adult. I am fascinated by the migration of the damsel nymph to the shoreline as it prepares to hatch into the winged adult," says stillwater specialist Rick Takahashi.

Damsel hatches get lake fishermen all fired up! They typically begin as early as late June, but July is prime time in most locations. Prior to emergence, fishing a damsel nymph from shore is as exciting as it gets. The nymphs swim toward the shore, where they'll crawl up on vegetation to emerge into adults. "I am intrigued by the side-to-side motion of a damsel nymph as it makes its way to the surface to hatch. I have studied the movement of the nymph, how it stops at intervals to rest before continuing on with its journey to the shore to hatch into an adult. This pause in a damsel's

Rick Takahashi's patterns capture every detail of the food organism he tries to imitate. Takahashi begins the process by collecting specimens and closely studying them, watching their behavior, and carefully scrutinizing their physical makeup. The end results are patterns like his Static Damsel, which stillwater enthusiasts have come to depend upon for matching the hatch on Colorado's lakes.

movement as it swims is what gave me the idea to design a damsel at rest."

Takahashi is a mastermind when it comes to designing flies. In an effort to create a realistic damsel nymph, he collected several specimens from lakes throughout Colorado. He closely scrutinized the nymphs to see what features he needed to include into his design. Through careful observation, Takahashi noticed that a damsel nymph would oftentimes have an arched abdomen when at rest. The challenge was to find a hook that simulated that posture. Takahashi decided that the swimming nymph hook manufactured by Daiichi (1770) was the perfect fit for his pattern.

Next, Takahashi studied the tail of the damsel nymph and came to the conclusion that it consisted of three paddlelike appendages. "I looked at several different materials to imitate the tail, including marabou and hen feathers, but found that ostrich herl tips would meet my needs. I liked the sturdiness of the stem of the ostrich herl and felt like the rounded shape of the tips would mimic the look of the caudal tail perfectly."

His next obstacle was to create an abdomen that incorporated the look of a segmented body with the dorsal (top side) of the abdomen a darker color than the underside. "I selected light-olive sewing thread to be used as the underbody and rib and placed a strip of light-olive Swiss Straw to act as the dorsal topping, bringing it forward to become part of the wing case and head of the damsel."

Takahashi incorporates olive Ice Dub into his design to form the thorax. He ties in an olive partridge feather with the center section clipped out, attaching the feather with the concave side facing the hook shank to create the legs. To form the eyes, Takahashi uses a piece of 25-pound monofilament with burnt ends to hold two olive, matte-finished glass beads in place.

Takahashi recommends fishing his Static Damsel close to shoreline in shallower water where you can see bottom, or near a drop-off. The fish face outward from the bank looking for swimming damsel nymphs that are heading toward the shore to emerge. "I use a slip strike indicator to suspend my damsel nymph. Oftentimes I use a damsel nymph as my lead fly, and then attach a dropper-fly (*Callibaetis* nymph, Chironomid, etc.) off the bend of the hook about 18 inches from the point fly. I cast the fly out as far as I can, or to where I see fish chasing damsel nymphs. I allow the fly to sink, remove any slack, then lower my rod tip to the surface of the water in line with the indicator. Then I begin retrieving the fly with short strips, causing the indicator to hop an inch or two, then I stop movement of the flies, wait a few seconds, then start a slow 'hand twist' retrieve. If nothing happens, I repeat the process, covering the water methodically. I can't stress enough the importance of using a slow retrieve. Most of the invertebrates in lakes don't move as fast as some think, so slow things down!"

Stillwater enthusiasts should fish their damsel nymphs close to the shoreline just beyond the littoral zone or drop-off. The color change in the substrate helps anglers identify the drop-off. LANDON MAYER

Steve's Stone

(Tied by Steve Thomas)

- **Hook:** #6–#12 Tiemco 5263
- **Thread:** 6/0 brown Uni-Thread
- **Underbody:** .020 lead wire
- **Tail:** Brown goose biots
- **Rib:** Red Ultra Wire (small)
- **Abdomen:** Dark hare's mask
- **Thorax:** Dark hare's mask
- **Wing case:** Brown Swiss Straw
- **Legs:** Natural pheasant tail fibers
- **Antennae:** Brown goose biots

Steve Thomas moved from Michigan to Colorado during the summer of 1976. When he got to the Rockies, one of his top priorities was to learn how to fish western rivers. "In the first few years I was in the West, I wanted to see and fish all the rivers. I didn't fish them all, but I am grateful that I had the opportunity to fish so many of them. One of my favorites was the Roaring Fork River in Colorado. The one thing I learned quickly: If I was going to be successful on Colorado rivers—freestones in particular—I was going to need a good stonefly pattern."

Over the years, I've tied my fair share stonefly patterns. Some of the super-realistic stonefly imitations can take up to 20 to 30 minutes to tie, which in many cases is a losing proposition. Many anglers are afraid to fish with realistic imitations for fear of losing them. I've given several of my friends some of my Paper Tiger Stonefly Nymphs, and they rarely fish them for obvious reasons.

Impressionistic patterns like Halfback Nymphs, Twenty Inchers, Bitch Creeks, Pat's Rubber Legs, and so on are proven favorites that often outperform exact imitations.

Steve's Stone is a buggy nymph that is tied with a blend of dark hare's mask dubbing. Thomas recommends mixing up your own batch of dubbing in a coffee grinder because you can control the amount of guard hairs that you use. The best guard hairs are found on the ears of the hare's mask. A well-tied Steve's Stone looks a bit on the messy side if you execute the dubbing correctly.

Per Thomas, "The impression of the fly in the water is the most important thing, not how they look in fly bins or in your hand. Steve's Stone came about from years of experimenting, reading, studying and working with a variety of tying materials, hook sizes and shapes, and, of course, many years of hard fishing."

I think Steve's Stone is so effective because it shares many similarities of a Hare's Ear. It's easy to tie, durable, and, like a Hare's Ear, its buggy appearance breathes life. Although Steve's Stone was originally designed for the Roaring Fork Valley, it fishes well on other freestones like the Colorado, Gunnison, Eagle, Conejos, Arkansas, and Animas Rivers and the Rio Grande because there is an abundant population of *Pteronarcys californica* stoneflies in those watersheds.

Pteronarcys californica, commonly referred to as salmon flies or willow flies, begin hatching during the first two weeks of June. In some watersheds, like the lower Colorado River near State Bridge, salmon flies can hatch as early as the last week of May. Steve's Stone is most effective on the front end of the hatch, when the nymphs are migrating toward the river's edge to emerge into adults. Emergence occurs on land, but the migratory phase, when heavy concentrations of nymphs are on the move, can provide some of the best nymph fishing of the year.

Salmon-fly hatches progress upstream each day, so being in the right place at the right time is critical for success. If you're on the leading edge of the hatch, fishing can be exceptional. But if you're in the thickest part of the hatch, the trout are often unwilling to eat because their stomachs are crammed full of stonefly nymphs. *Pteronarcys californica* may live up to 4 years before reaching maturity, so it is important to understand that even after the adults have emerged for the season, several year classes of stonefly nymphs remain plentiful in the stream.

Steve's Stone should be fished with a conventional nymphing rig, consisting of a 9-foot tapered leader terminating in 4X tippet. Add an additional 18 inches of 4X tippet to extend the life of your leader. Attach a number 4 split shot above the knot that joins the leader and tippet to help the fly sink abruptly. Steve's Stone is weighted, so don't get carried away with too much lead. Don't rule out using two stonefly nymphs, spaced 12 to 14 inches apart, during peak emergence. Make sure to concentrate your efforts along the stream bank, where the trout are stacked up, keying heavily on stonefly nymphs as they prepare to crawl on land.

During other times of the year, it's never a bad idea to use Steve's Stone as an attractor and trail a mayfly imitation like a Barr's Emerger, Mitchell's Split Case, Bead Head Flashback Pheasant Tail, or a Sparkle Wing RS 2 behind it. Even during the winter, it doesn't hurt to think outside the box from time to time and dredge a stonefly nymph in a deep hole. Opportunistic trout are aware of their presence and rarely waste any time grabbing a big bite if the opportunity presents itself.

Stoneflies thrive in fast-oxygenated trout streams like the Roaring Fork River. Steve's Stone has been a proven producer in the Roaring Fork Valley for over four decades.

Top Secret Midge

(Tied by Pat Dorsey)

- **Hook:** #18–#26 Tiemco 2488
- **Thread:** Dark-brown 8/0 Uni-Thread
- **Rib:** White 6/0 Uni-Thread
- **Wing:** Prism White Glamour Madeira
- **Thorax:** Rust-brown Superfine

The Top Secret Midge is a pattern I designed during the winter of 2001. In its embryonic form, my goal was to create a realistic midge pupa to imitate the millions of midges that hatch daily on the South Platte watershed. Strange as it might sound, the Top Secret Midge's name was an afterthought—a spur-of-the-moment decision that came about while a group of guides were out enjoying a day off on the South Platte River near the small community of Deckers. I had hooked and landed a handful of nice brown trout in a riffle-run-pool tailout, several hundred yards above the

Trumbull Bridge, when Mick Stefan, one of my colleagues, asked me what pattern I was catching my fish on.

You have to know Stefan to appreciate this—he's always joking around about something. I looked at Stefan and told him I was using a "Top Secret Midge." Stefan gave me one of the strangest looks that I have ever seen, a puzzled expression, and deep inside you could see the wheels were spinning trying to figure it out.

Truth be told, I was hooking and landing trout on a new midge imitation I had not named yet. It was quickly becoming one of

The Top Secret Midge has become a staple for tailwater enthusiasts. The brown-and-white segmented thread body closely mimics a midge's abdomen, while the bulbous thorax that contains the wings and legs of the emerging adult are imitated with brown Superfine dubbing and Glamour Madeira. The Glamour Madeira wing produces a "dash of flash" that attracts nearby trout during the height of a midge hatch.

my go-to patterns because I was consistently fooling selective trout in Eleven Mile Canyon, Cheesman Canyon, and Deckers with it. "Come on—what are you using?" Stefan asked. I told him a "Top Secret Midge," chuckled a bit, then proceeded to show him the fly. He flipped down his magnification aid on the brim of his hat and stared at my little brown midge pupa with amazement. "Can you spare a couple of those?" Stefan asked. I gave him a few, and from that moment on, the pattern was called the Top Secret Midge.

Over the past two decades, the Top Secret Midge has become a Colorado favorite, fooling selective trout on both the state's world-class tailwaters and renowned freestone streams. I recommend carrying the Top Secret Midge in a wide range of sizes from a size 18 down to a 26. During the spring months a size 18 is deadly for imitating the big spring midge, which begins hatching in mid- to late March and continues through the first part of April. The summer season requires a slightly different approach, using smaller imitations (sizes

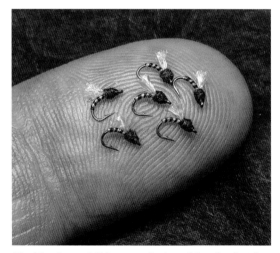

The Top Secret Midge was designed for the finicky trout that reside on the South Platte River. It is tied on a Tiemco 2488, which is a 3X wide, 2X short hook, which assists in a good hookup-to-landing ratio even on the smallest of sizes.

20–22) to match the hatch. During the winter (Nov–Mar) anglers need to downsize their midge nymphs even more. Oftentimes, the difference between catching fish and not catching fish is using a size 24 or 26 instead of a 22.

The Top Secret Midge can be tied in a wide array of colors. Some of my favorites include red, fluorescent green, black, and purple. I've found that the red variation works well for imitating blood midges, and the bright green version is a great candidate for mimicking the lime green midges that hatch on many of our tailwaters. Purple is the new rage in trout flies, so it made complete sense to tie some up. And you can never go wrong with something that is small and black when it comes to imitating midge pupae. I recommend using a black rib on the red and bright green Top Secret Midges, and a white rib on the purple and black variations.

The most effective method to fish your Top Secret Midge is on the dead drift with a conventional two- or three-fly nymphing rig composed of a 9-foot tapered leader, terminating in 6X tippet. Off an attractor (red larva, micro egg, flashy midge, etc.), tie an additional piece of 6X tippet (14–16 inches in length for a two-fly rig or 8–10 inches for a three-fly rig) off the bend or eye of the hook and attach another small midge larva or pupa. Repeat this process for the third fly if you opt to use one.

I use the Top Secret Midge (a pupa imitation) as my trailer in my tandem nymphing rigs, as it should naturally ride higher in the water column to match the naturals. Complete your nymphing rig by attaching a yarn strike indicator, keeping it twice the depth of the river's substrate, and a #4 or #6 split shot 12 inches above the upper fly. I fine-tune my weight with JP's Nymphing Mud to get my flies in the correct feeding zone. Too much weight can be as problematic as not enough during the height of the hatch.

Tungsten Pyrite Caddis

(Tied by Eric Pettine)

- **Hook:** #14–#18 Tiemco 2488
- **Bead:** Black tungsten followed by chartreuse (3.0 mm for #14 and 2.5 mm for #16–#18)
- **Thread:** Black 70 denier Ultra Thread
- **Abdomen:** Gray muskrat
- **Overbody:** Black hackle, palmered and clipped
- **Rib:** Gold Lagartun oval tinsel (small)
- **Legs:** Whiting Farms black rooster hackle

Longtime fishing guide and master fly tier Eric Pettine of Fort Collins, Colorado, originated the Tungsten Pyrite Caddis back in the late 1960s. According to Pettine, "This fly has a long history, and it evolved slowly. When I left the Air Force in Alaska in 1969 and settled my family in Fort Collins, Colorado, I adopted the Poudre River as my home water. I needed a nymph that would work there, so tied a pattern with a muskrat body and a black fur head. It worked pretty well, but I felt it lacked something."

While Pettine was elk hunting on Cameron Pass the following fall, he realized that he hadn't brought enough water. Pettine was desperately thirsty, so he risked getting giardiasis by drinking out of a little stream. As he lowered his face to drink some water, he noticed a bunch of caddis larvae on a rock. Their cases glittered with iron pyrite. That's when he realized that his caddisfly needed tinsel to imitate the sparkle in the case.

"We did not have beads available yet, so my fishing buddy and I agreed that the black head

Eric Pettine's Tungsten Pyrite Caddis evolved over time into one of his favorite cased caddis imitations. Modern-day advancements with fly-tying materials and streamside observation aided in the progression. The final product is a stunning, realistic Brachycentrus *imitation that catches trout in just about any watershed in Colorado.*

of a caddis larva should be tied out of Angus underfur. A rancher nearby had a herd of Black Angus cattle, so we decided to go out and pick fur off the barbed-wire fence around his pasture. One day the rancher came by and asked what we were doing. We explained our need for the black fur to tie flies. He said, go into the pasture. That scratching post is full of fur."

The rancher warned Pettine about the bull that was in the pasture. Apparently he was quite aggressive and would chase people from time to time. "One evening after work, my fishing partner and I decided to go collect a bag of fur, but it had gotten dark on our way out. Carelessly, I walked up on the bull, lying down and nearly invisible in the long grass. He jumped up with a snort. I ran for the fence. I almost cleared the top wire of the barbed fence, but my left leg got hung up on my jeans and I tumbled to the ground. I thought I could hear the bull chuckling. After that we decided that black rabbit fur worked just fine." Behind the head, Pettine used a small band of caddis green dubbing to imitate the larva inside the

Eric Pettine's Tungsten Pyrite Caddis is perfect for western trout streams like the Williams Fork because it sinks quickly in the swift currents. Both the Williams Fork and nearby Colorado River are known for their exceptional caddis hatches.

case with a few turns of black rooster hackle to simulate legs.

When beads became available, Pettine replaced the black fur with a black tungsten bead and swapped out the caddis green dubbing with a chartreuse bead. The beads also helped with the fly's sink rate. Pettine also added a clipped black hackle over the body. Pettine was convinced that stubble on the abdomen made the fly look and feel like a rough caddis case (*Brachycentrus*) to the trout. The end result was a fly that fooled trout on all the rivers he fished, even the Frying Pan, which is a true testament.

"My favorite place to use Tungsten Pyrite Caddis is in pocket water. Most of my casts there are 30 feet or less. That means that with a 9-foot leader, I only have about 20 feet of fly line out on the water. After 74 years of fly fishing, I predate a strike indicator by 40 years or so, especially in pocket water, so I never use a strike indicator. After I cast the fly, I can see the tip of my line-leader connection and even knots in my leader. I also often see the fish take the fly. An indicator would be a distraction from all the good stuff going on. I keep the tip of the line and about a foot of leader greased with floatant so that it rides high. I like fishing straight upstream, making two or three casts—no more—to likely spots, searching for feeding fish, then move on to the next pocket. I don't like to waste time on fish that are not feeding. When I was young, I would cover a lot of water this way. Often, I hitchhiked back to my truck, which was sometimes 2 miles away. I remember once fishing the Blue River with Ken Walters, an eastern boy who would find a good run and fish there all day. When I returned 5 hours later, he said, 'You're not a fly fisher, you're a hiker!' I admit that he caught as many fish as I did, but staying in one run all day is not my style."

Two Bit Hooker

(Tied by Charlie Craven)

- **Hook:** #14–#18 Tiemco 3769
- **Bead:** Two ³⁄₃₂" copper tungsten
- **Threads:** Red 70 denier UTC and black 14/0 Veevus
- **Tail:** Mottled India Hen saddle fibers
- **Abdomen:** Red 70 denier UTC tying thread
- **Rib:** Black 14/0 Veevus thread
- **Wing case:** Medium Opal Mirage tinsel
- **Thorax:** Mahogany Superfine dubbing
- **Legs:** Mottled India Hen saddle fibers
- **Coating:** Solarez Thin Hard UV Resin

Dry-and-droppers are a nice alternative to conventional nymph-fishing rigs, especially in shallow riffles, transitional zones, and along the edges of streams, where fish become sensitive to overhead threats. A fly that sinks fast but has a realistic profile is important when you are choosing a nymph to be suspended off a large, beefy dry fly.

Charlie Craven's Two Bit Hooker has become a Colorado favorite—especially for float anglers who pound the stream banks with dry-and-droppers on freestone streams like the Arkansas, Roaring Fork, Gunnison,

Colorado, and Animas Rivers and the Rio Grande. The Two Bit Hooker is equally effective on smaller streams if you downsize it a bit and drop it off an Elk Hair Caddis, Parachute Adams, or Yellow Stimulator.

"The Two Bit Hooker is personally my most commonly fished pattern. I came up with the idea for this fly many years ago on the way home from an Arkansas River float with my friend Larry Friedrichs. The drive home from a trip is always ripe with fly ideas as the miles roll by on the highway and my mind is free to wander. I wanted a pattern to fish in a

Flies that sink quick have become popular in recent years. Charlie Craven's Two Bit Hooker incorporates two tungsten beads into the design in comparison to most bead-head patterns that only use one. The Two Bit Hooker is a nice option for anglers who enjoy fishing with dry-and-dropper rigs, especially from drift boats or inflatable rafts.

dry-and-dropper rig that was still small and proportioned but really heavy! I played with way too many ideas before it finally dawned on me to use two, rather than one, tungsten beads. This double-tungsten-beaded fly is tied with a smooth, slick thread body and soft hen saddle fiber legs and tail, all with very little resistance to sinking, and has my signature UV resin top coat to add toughness and shape. The combination of materials makes it quick and easy to tie, and the fly gets down right now and stays there where the fish are."

In a variety of colors and sizes, the Two Bit Hooker can match just about any mayfly hatch in Colorado. Craven recommends tying the Two Bit Hooker in sizes 12 to 18 in red, brown, purple, hot pink, light olive, dark olive, and black. Each color has a time and place. For instance, dark olive in smaller sizes is perfect for *Baetis* nymphs, but in larger sizes, it doubles as a green drake nymph. Light olive is good for imitation PMD nymphs in July and early August, and so on. Some of the brighter colors (hot pink, purple, red) work well during non-hatch periods, when trout are looking to feed opportunistically.

"The Two Bit Hooker is a perfect dry-and-dropper nymph that finds its way to the end of my line at some point during every one of my fishing trips." Craven believes that one of the reasons his fly works so well is that it hangs taut on the dropper, down deep, and eliminates slack in the tippet between the dry and the nymph, making bites show up on the dry fly (indicator) almost instantly. "Flies that aren't as heavy allow that bit of slack, and slack is the devil in a dry-and-dropper rig. Shun that devil and you too shall be rewarded."

On float trips Craven likes to tie on a size 14 red Two Bit Hooker, trailed off a 3-foot-long 4X dropper attached to the bend of a Charlie Boy Hopper. "I usually end up with the rod bent most of the day. In smaller water a size 18 black or brown version is extremely effective under a smaller dry fly like a Parachute Adams. If I found myself at the river having left my box of Two Bits at home, I can honestly say I'd just turn around and go back and get it."

If you find that a Two Bit Hooker is getting hung up in shallow water, try Craven's Jujubaetis, another popular pattern to imitate small mayflies. The weight of the UV resin used on the wing pad helps the fly sink into the correct part of the feeding zone. Craven offers this bit of advice on his Jujubaetis: "The top coat finishes off the shape of the fly into that perfect teardrop profile so reminiscent of a small mayfly nymph and adds a bit of weight, a lot of durability, and about 3 pounds of curbside appeal to an already incredibly effective fly. I tie the Jujubaetis in sizes 16 to 22 in a bunch of color combinations."

If you're a big fan of the Two Bit Hooker, you'll love its cousin, the Two Bit Stone. Craven ties it in sizes 8 to 16 to imitate golden stoneflies and sizes 12 to 18 for Yellow Sally stoneflies with all the same goals in mind.

Mark Adams and Jason Booth teamed up to catch this Gunnison River brown trout on a size 16 olive Two Bit Hooker. Two Bit Hookers are a great option for anglers who enjoy floating some of the state's larger freestone streams with dry-and-dropper rigs.

UV Scud

(Tied by Pat Dorsey)

- **Hook:** #12–#18 Tiemco 2457
- **Thread:** Orange Danville 6/0
- **Tail:** Orange Antron
- **Rib:** 4X monofilament
- **Shell back:** Ziplock bag strip
- **Abdomen:** Shrimp-pink UV Ice Dub
- **Antennae:** Orange Antron

May and June comprise the high-water season in Colorado, but don't let that fool you: Spring runoff can provide some of the best nymph fishing of the year, especially with shrimplike crustaceans known as scuds. Your scud selection should consist of several different colors—light and dark olive, tan, and orange—because they each play a unique role in fooling trout.

My seine samples indicate that the majority of scuds found in rivers and streams are some shade of olive and have a brilliant UV sheen to them. On occasion, I find a tan one in my sample, which is a good indication that I'm looking at a scud that has recently molted. When scuds die they turn orange quickly, so make sure you carry plenty of offerings that resemble dead scuds.

I designed the UV Scud back in the mid-1990s to imitate one of the most important food sources for tailwater trout. All Colorado fly fishers should familiarize themselves with two different genera: *Gammarus* and *Hyalella*. *Gammarus* is the larger of the two scuds, ranging in size from 10 to 25 mm. *Hyalella* is its smaller cousin, which typically

May and June typically produce some of the best scud fishing of the year in Cheesman Canyon and Deckers. Fluctuating flows, especially when the river levels are on the rise, are a great time to fish with an orange UV Scud. I recommend using larger sizes (#12–#14) during the onset of spring runoff but switching to smaller scud imitations (#16–#18) when the flow stabilizes and begins to recede.

ranges from 3 to 5 mm. Scuds do not have a complicated life cycle—they begin their life as small scuds and die as large scuds, which really simplifies things. In a wide range of colors and sizes (#12–#18), you can imitate both species without a lot of effort.

The UV Scud's design is simple but effective. I begin by clamping a scud hook into my vise and lashing a piece of Antron (orange, olive, or tan) across the top of the hook shank to imitate the tail and antennae. The shellback is a plastic strip cut from a ziplock bag. Monofilament is used for the rib, which helps punctuate the segmentation in the shellback, giving it that "true crustacean look."

The body is made from UV Ice Dub in shrimp pink (actually looks orange), light yellow, or light green. The UV dubbing is one of the most important components of the fly design because it produces the lifelike translucency. Shrimp pink is recommended for imitating dead scuds, light yellow is perfect for mimicking newly molted scuds, and the light olive is ideal for replicating living scuds.

After dubbing the body, the shellback is pulled over and secured near the eye of the

The high-water season provides tailwater enthusiasts with some exceptional nymph fishing with orange UV scuds. This thick-bodied brown trout was fooled near Deckers when outflows from Cheesman Reservoir were at 450 cfs.

hook, then ribbed with seven or eight turns of monofilament. I clip off the excess shellback and monofilament and bury the butt ends with a few wraps of tying thread. The final step is to use a bodkin to pull the dubbing down to form legs. Trim the dubbing (legs) parallel with the bottom of the hook to complete the fly. I tie them in sizes 12 to 18, but 14s and 16s are my top producers.

Stillwater enthusiasts should carry a thorough selection of scuds because they are important a large percentage of the year. Scuds thrive in weed-rich alkaline lakes and have a substantial impact on a trout's growth rate in places like Antero, Spinney Mountain, and Delaney Buttes. It's hard to go wrong with a size 10-to-12 olive scud (*Gammarus*) on any one of the previously mentioned stillwater impoundments when you are fishing near a weed bed or drop-off.

In moving water, olive scuds fish well year-round because opportunistic trout are always looking for them. Scuds often become victims of behavioral drift, so fishing them during low light (dawn and dusk) is usually a good strategy. Make no mistake about it—the best scud fishing occurs during higher flow regimes or periods of extreme fluctuation, when discharge rates change daily to meet downstream irrigation demand. Trout frequently take an orange scud as an egg in many tailraces, because the rainbow trout often spawn until the latter part of May due to the ice-cold water temperatures.

I recommend fishing a scud in a tandem nymphing rig, using the scud as an attractor, and trailing a smaller fly behind it that matches the prevailing hatch. For instance, if I'm fishing a scud during the winter, I'll trail a midge pupa; if it's April, May, or June, I'll opt to trail a *Baetis* nymph; and so on. As a general rule, I fish scuds mid-column to imitate the naturals that have been swept away from the substrate (weed beds) and drift helpless in the current.

WD-40

(Tied by Mark Engler)

- **Hook:** #18–#22 Tiemco 2487
- **Thread:** Brown 8/0 Uni-Thread
- **Tail:** Mallard flank or lemon wood duck
- **Abdomen:** Brown 8/0 Uni-Thread
- **Thorax:** Rust-brown Supefine dubbing
- **Wing case:** Mallard flank or lemon wood duck

Mark Engler's WD-40 is a must-have for any tailwater enthusiast. In a wide array of colors and sizes, the WD-40 is a simple yet effective pattern that imitates both midge pupae and *Baetis* nymphs. Engler grew up fishing Colorado tailwaters, which taught him how to fool difficult trout at an early age. His favorite tailraces included the Frying Pan River and the South Platte River below Cheesman Reservoir.

"I routinely fished Cheesman Canyon top to bottom. I parked my truck in the lower parking lot and rode my minibike up to the parking lot near the dam. I would start fishing near the gauging station and work my way to the lower canyon. After a long day of fishing, I would hike out of the lower canyon, then drive my truck back up to the dam to get my minibike."

Engler also spent several weeks a year in the Glenwood Springs Valley fishing the "Pan" and routinely hung out at Roy Palm's Frying Pan Angler. "I probably drove Roy Palm nuts, but he was always willing to help me out and support my addiction. He was even kind enough to buy flies from me while I was going to college at Adams State University in Alamosa.

Anglers have come to depend on Mark Engler's WD-40 to fool selective trout that are feeding on midge pupa and Baetis *nymphs. The WD-40 is easy to tie, extremely durable, and consistently catches trout day in and day out.*

Once I graduated from college, Roy Palm convinced me to become a fishing guide." Engler started his guiding career for Abe and Tim Chavez (Abe's Fly Shop in Navajo Dam, New Mexico) in 1989 and worked there until 1991.

The WD-40 originated on the Frying Pan out of necessity to imitate "gorilla midges" (what we call the big spring midge on the South Platte River) that hatch mid-March through the first part of April. Engler's midge imitation incorporated a sparse tail, thin abdomen, and small ball of dubbing in the thorax to simulate a midge pushing its way out of its shuck. At the time, Engler's concoction did not have a name, so he asked Abe Chavez what he should call it. Chavez said, "Lets call it the Wet Dream—you fish it wet and it works like a dream. It routinely catches forty fish a day, so let's call it the WD-40."

In 1992 Engler went to work for Duranglers, a fly shop and guide service that specializes in fooling selective trout all over southwest Colorado and the San Juan River below Navajo Dam. Nearly 30 years later, he is still one of Duranglers senior guides and resides in Bayfield, Colorado.

His colleagues at Duranglers speak highly of the WD-40. "Over the past 20-odd years, the WD-40 nymph rose to prominence as one of the most effective flies for catching midge and blue-winged olive eating trout. Across Colorado and the Rocky Mountain West, the WD-40 is a simple fly that many a tailwater guide has come to rely on. It is an extremely quick and easy tie, and any tier should be able to crank out a dozen or more in an hour."

Engler's original WD-40 pattern was tied with a 2X heavy nymph hook with olive 6/0 Danville thread. After clamping the hook into the vise, Engler recommends attaching the thread behind the eye of the hook and wrapping it rearward with symmetrical wraps toward hook bend. For the tail Engler suggests

using mallard flank feather, off the wing, not the leg, as he feels the wing flank feather is much stronger. The tail length should be about a shank length long.

Engler likes to seat the tail with a couple loose wraps of thread and warns tiers that the tail will break off if you get the thread too tight. After the tail is secured in place near the hook bend, he advances the thread forward covering up the mallard flank, leaving the thread at the ¾ point on the hook shank. Engler pulls back the mallard flank and stands the feather up with a thread wedge (several

This brown trout ate a size-20 brown Flashback WD-40 during the initial stages of a blue-winged olive hatch. Trailing a brown WD-40 off another Baetis *nymph stacks the odds in your favor when the trout begin to feed selectively on mayfly nymphs and emergers.*

wraps of tying thread), which is used for the wing case. Engler prefers to use natural chocolate rabbit fur for the thorax, dubbing it pretty loose, then pulling the mallard flank forward to form the wing case. He secures the mallard flank in place with three or four turns of thread, then double whip-finishes the head to complete the fly.

Most WD-40s you see in fly bins and anglers' fly boxes today are tied on a Tiemco 2487. Engler admits he currently likes to use the curved shank (Tiemco 2487) for midges and the straight hook (Tiemco 3769) for *Baetis* nymphs. Popular colors include black, brown, gray, and olive in sizes 18 to 24. The tail, thread abdomen, and wing case design has stayed the same over the years, but most tiers prefer Superfine dubbing for the thorax because it has less guard hairs and is easier to use. I like using lemon wood duck flank feathers instead of mallard (that is, if you can get your hands on some) because the feathers are higher quality, which ties better-looking and more consistent flies in my humble opinion.

Most anglers fish a WD-40 underneath a strike indicator in a tandem nymphing rig, with 9-foot leader terminating in 6X tippet. The WD-40 is a perfect dropper, trailed off an attractor nymph. The WD-40 is a good choice when trout are keying midge pupae or blue-winged olive emergers mid-column. I can honestly say I that I have caught fish on every one of the previously mentioned colors, but brown is no doubt my top producer.

There have been many variations of the WD-40 that have surfaced over the years, including a flashback version where a strip of Mylar tinsel is swapped out for the mallard flank feather, and Boomer Stout's WD-50, which has a flashback and emerging wing, and several tungsten bead-head varieties. Duranglers says that "variations of the WD-40 are just fine, it is the natural progression of fly tying and it is a good thing. I would hate to ask how many Copper John variations there actually are." But it's important to give credit where credit is due, and Mark Engler's original WD-40 is no doubt one of Colorado's favorite flies.

Zing Wing Midge

(Tied by Jim Cannon)

- **Hook:** #18–#24 Tiemco 101
- **Abdomen:** Black 8/0 Uni-Thread
- **Wing/wing case:** Bett's Zing Wing
- **Thorax:** Black Superfine
- **Legs:** Black Z-Lon

I had the pleasure of meeting John Betts for the first time back in the mid-1990s on a routine visit to The Flyfisher in Cherry Creek. I was delivering some Bead Head Breadcrust and Paper Tiger Stonefly nymphs that Ken Walters ordered for his inventory. Walters was kind enough to introduce us and strike up a casual conversation. It was an honor to finally meet Betts because I had heard so many wonderful things about him from Jim Cannon, my boss at the time at the Blue Quill Angler in Evergreen, Colorado.

Jim Cannon was kind enough to share this interesting story about Betts. "My career in fly fishing began in 1985 when I started tying flies and selling them to several local fly shops in Denver. I was running a shelter for the homeless in Denver and needed some extra income to support my growing fly-fishing hobby. The Flyfisher, then located at 232 Nelson Street in Cherry Creek, was one of my accounts. Ken Walters was the owner and Mike Clough, who later became my Orvis rep, was the manager. I would come in and Clough would give me

John Betts was one of the most innovative fly designers of our time. Betts will forever be known for his creativity and the use of synthetic materials. The Zing Wing Midge incorporates two of his most popular tying materials into the design: Zing Wing and Z-Lon.

a fly sample. I would get the materials then start tying the order. When browsing through their bins, I noticed a grouping of flies that was dedicated and tied by a man named John Betts. There were never many flies in the bins, as they were bought up quickly, and I am sure Betts couldn't keep up with the demand. I was fascinated by the Betts fly patterns. They were all tied with synthetic materials and were anatomically perfect. His Tyvec caddis pattern was mottled and had antennae. His Trico spinner had three perfectly divided tails made out of synthetic paintbrush. The Trico spinners were tied in black and olive to imitate males and females. His mayfly duns—PMD, blue-winged olive, and red quill—were tied with a Z-Lon Comparadun-style wing and were perfect in coloration and size. His stonefly nymph had six legs, three Tyvek wing cases, two tails, and two antennae. The body was made out of strips of rubber dental dam that gave perfect segmentation and taper to the body. They looked like they could crawl out of the fly bins."

John Betts's Zing Wing Midge is the perfect imposter to imitate the big spring midge that begins hatching in mid-March and continues through the first part of April. In flight, many anglers confuse the big spring midge for a blue-winged olive because of its enormous size. Further inspection, especially when they are at rest or crawling on snow, reveal they are truly adult midges because their wings lie straight back over their abdomen.

Cannon went on to explain that he felt that Betts was in a league of his own because his patterns were innovative, entomologically correct, and, most of all, tied perfectly! Cannon's dream was to learn how to tie flies from the master himself. "I contacted Betts and asked him if he would teach me how to tie his patterns. He agreed to mentor me under one condition: When we were through, I would buy him a Winston 9-foot, 5-weight fly rod. I agreed to his terms and we began the tying sessions.

We didn't tie specific patterns at first. Betts taught me how to tie different types of tails, then bodies, then wings, legs, antennae, and so on. Then he taught me how to put them all together. Betts taught me about dubbing, how to blend it, how to feel it, and how to make a noodle so small you could make a #26 dubbed thorax on a midge using the "touch dubbing" technique with fly-tying wax. Betts instructed me how to tie in MicroFibbets to make a divided Comparadun-style outrigger tail, and then how to get a perfectly divided three-fiber tail for Trico spinners. He taught me that on small flies, every wrap of thread should have a purpose. Betts stressed the importance of proportioning and the amount of material put on a fly, that less is often better. After learning Betts's techniques, it was much easier to tie the finished product."

Betts's Zing Wing Midge is a local favorite for many die-hard dry-fly enthusiasts that frequent the South Platte River in Cheesman Canyon and the nearby Deckers stretch. As Cannon mentioned, Betts believed that "less is more," and his Zing Wing Midge is a great example of that. The abdomen is tied with uniform and symmetrical wraps of tying thread, the wing and wing case are constructed from Zing Wing, and the legs are made from Z-Lon. The thorax is composed of a few fibers of Superfine dubbing. Simple but effective!